Living Your Best Life
While Embracing Christianity

Living Your Best Life

While Embracing Christianity

If Not Now, When?

Sherry Koppal-Gilmore

XULON PRESS

Xulon Press
555 Winderley Pl, Suite 225
Maitland, FL 32751
407.339.4217
www.xulonpress.com

© 2024 by Sherry Koppal-Gilmore

All rights reserved solely by the author. The author guarantees all contents are original and do not infringe upon the legal rights of any other person or work. No part of this book may be reproduced in any form without the permission of the author.

Due to the changing nature of the Internet, if there are any web addresses, links, or URLs included in this manuscript, these may have been altered and may no longer be accessible. The views and opinions shared in this book belong solely to the author and do not necessarily reflect those of the publisher. The publisher therefore disclaims responsibility for the views or opinions expressed within the work.

Unless otherwise indicated, Scripture quotations taken from the Holy Bible, New Living Translation (NLT). Copyright ©1996, 2004, 2007 by Tyndale House Foundation. Used by permission of Tyndale House Publishers, Inc.

Unless otherwise indicated, Scripture quotations taken from the Holy Bible, New International Version (NIV). Copyright © 1973, 1978, 1984, 2011 by Biblica, Inc.™. Used by permission. All rights reserved.

Unless otherwise indicated, Scripture quotations taken from the Living Bible (TLB). Copyright © 1971 by Tyndale House Foundation. Used by permission of Tyndale House Publishers Inc., Carol Stream, Illinois 60188. All rights reserved.

Unless otherwise indicated, Scripture quotations taken from the English Standard Version (ESV). Copyright © 2001 by Crossway, a publishing ministry of Good News Publishers. Used by permission. All rights reserved.

Unless otherwise indicated, Scripture quotations taken from The Good News Translation (GNT). Copyright © 1992 American Bible Society. Used by permission. All rights reserved.

Paperback ISBN-13: 979-8-86850-413-6
Dust Jacket ISBN-13: 979-8-86850-414-3
Ebook ISBN-13: 979-8-86850-415-0

Contents

Acknowledgments ix
Introduction xi

Section I: Getting to Know Yourself 1
1. Happiness: It's Yours If You Want It! 5
2. Snapshots of Life: Understanding the Life Cycle 21
3. Your Past: Perspectives Influencing Your Future. 35

Section II: Dreams and Making Them a Reality 49
4. The Bucket List: Adding Sprinkles to Your Life 53
5. Vision Boards: Manifesting Your Dreams 79
6. Setting Goals: Turning Your Dreams Into Reality 101

Section III: Getting What You Want by Taking Charge. . . .123
7. Time Management: Taking Charge of Your Life. 127
8. Living With Intention: Seizing Opportunities 149
9. The Comfort Zone: Practicing Emotional Yoga 169

Section IV: Glorifying The Lord .191
10. Embracing Relationships: Blessing Others 195
11. Living in God's Will: Listening to the Lord. 217
12. Are We There Yet: Enjoying the Journey. 231

Notes. 249
About the Author 261

Acknowledgments

I want to thank the many people who supported me in the writing of this book.

Rachel Cardona, Sally Dodson, Albert Garza, Stephanie Kreider, Kimberly Perez, Raquel Ruvo, and Jill Underbrink thank you so much for participating in my vision board workshop, reading my rough drafts, and giving me your honest feedback regarding my writing.

Kathleen Stines-Thorne and Kevin Thorne, thank you for your support, the sharing of your stories, and the pictures of your adventures.

Monica Wysong, thank you for being my editor and please know *that* you were a great help in getting me through the most frustrating part of publishing this book. I am so grateful for the encouragement you gave me when I felt too tired to go on. Thank you for not allowing me to give up at 90%.

My life group leaders Cylinder Bogk and Laurie Witt, thank you for your feedback regarding the spiritual message I wanted to convey and providing me with encouragement.

My Pastor, Reverend John Roberts, thank you for your spiritual guidance. The advice you have given me is priceless.

Carol Koppal—my mom! Thank you for being my rock!

Introduction

Thank you for picking up this book. I feel both honored and humbled that you will be reading my strategies for maximizing the enjoyment of your life. Together we will create an action plan for fulfilling your dreams. We will also explore how God has plans for your future.

This book is written from a Christian perspective. I want to live my life to the fullest, to have purpose, and to make a difference in this world. In order to accomplish this, deliberate actions must be taken. I have loved ones who I know without a doubt are in Heaven, and although we know a person cannot earn their way through those pearly gates, I am trying my best to ensure I get there as well. I hope you will join me in this journey to explore an exciting and meaningful life as a Christ follower.

My number one role in life is being a Christian. Am I a perfect child of God? Nope! I struggle just like everyone else. I still have work to do. No one is a perfect Christian and even when we improve, things will happen to derail us. The enemy attacks us more diligently the closer we get to the Lord, but do not allow this to sabotage your efforts at having a close relationship with God.

This book is about living your life to the fullest while embracing Christianity. We will talk about bucket list adventures, fulfilling dreams, and setting life goals as I reinforce

Living Your Best Life While Embracing Christianity

our discussion with Scripture. It has been a comforting process and made me more intentional about fulfilling my own dreams while honoring God.

Publishing a book has been both on my bucket list and a life goal. When I finally decided to make it a reality, I felt the Lord tugging on my heart. I had no idea how close I would feel to Him as I gathered scripture to support my statements.

This book is geared toward Christians who want to fulfill their dreams. Please, if you are a Christian reading this book, my intent is for you to pass it on to someone who may not know the love and power of Christ. My hope is that this book will be read for the initial content and one's faith will be awakened through the Scriptures. I guess every Christian writer has the goal of bringing a non-Christian to Christ through their work. In doing this, we must live our lives in a manner reflecting our belief and love of God. I have chosen to demonstrate my beliefs and love of the Lord through the writing of this book. With that being said, I am not an expert on Scripture. I researched scriptures that supported the topics I was discussing and tried to keep them within context, but we all know how statements can become misconstrued. So, I encourage you to delve deeper into the Word with those passages that resonate with you. I hope my interpretation of the Scriptures sparks further inquiry within you. I expect this book to give you many questions to ponder both regarding your life choices as well as Biblical commands. The Bible is complicated. It is the number one best-selling book, yet many people have never read the Bible in its entirety. I encourage you to do so. There are many one- and two-year formats that can help you in doing this. Please know

Introduction

I have done my best to present encouraging material with support from Scripture to guide you in living your best life in a Christian manner. I have prayed over this content and recommend you do so as well. Please know that God loves you and he is on your side.

♡

Sherry

Section I

Getting To Know Yourself

What does living your best life mean? We hear the phrase all the time. In living your best life, the focus is on the fact that this is your own unique life. You are responsible for how your life turns out. You enter this world with a particular family background and socioeconomic status. Your dreams and talents are distinctive all unto you. That is what makes you so special. Living your best life includes feeling confident in who you are and being decisive about what you want. It means you have the attitude of gratitude, appreciating what you have, and making the most of your current season of life. Living your best life means whether you are eighteen or eighty, you have goals to strive for. You have people in your life who you love and care for, who also love and care for you. Most importantly, if you are living your best life, you have a personal relationship with Jesus Christ and live your life as a means of worshiping Him.

In section I of this book you will discover which stage of life you are currently in, as well as how your perspective of your past influences your future. We will explore what happiness means to you. You will learn how to identify and clarify what exactly you want out of life.

Heavenly Father,

Please bless us with your guidance as we read through this book. Provide us with the insight to make the necessary changes in our lives so we can live the life of enjoyment and fulfillment that you intended for us. Help us to remain humble as we reach our life goals. Remind us to be a blessing to others along the way. Thank you for this opportunity to mature as a person and grow closer to You.

Amen

"Some people want it to happen, some wish it would happen, others make it happen."

- Michael Jordan

Chapter 1

Happiness
It's Yours if You Want It!

Smiles and laughter. Adventure and success. Sunshine and friendship. Surrounded by loved ones with not a care in the world. It's the way people portray themselves on social media. It's what we all strive for. We even question ourselves when we are not in a constant state of it. Happiness is seen as a goal in life. Why do some people have it while others do not? Can you achieve happiness? Yes, you can. Happiness is attainable. Happiness is a choice we make.

What is Happiness?

Happiness comes in several forms. It's that feeling there is no place you would rather be. Enjoying life in the moment. It's looking around and finding you truly appreciate and delight in the company of the people you are with. Another form of happiness is that feeling of elation at an accomplishment completed. How about that feeling of exhilaration when you have had a recent adventure? We know it when we experience it. Happiness is a positive emotion. "Happiness...", according to Reverend John Roberts (Grace Presbyterian Church) "...doesn't come from outer circumstances, it comes from the inside." Happiness is not a constant state of being. Some people can hold onto this feeling, while for others, it is merely a fleeting experience. I want you to be able to experience lasting happiness in your life.

Happiness is a choice

As stated above, happiness is a choice, and despite what the media will tell you, it will take some work. Honestly, happiness starts with God. If we have a life in which we know the Lord has our back, then there is nothing we can't do. It's a glorious feeling to know that as we go through life, with its ups and downs, the people who enter and leave our lives, along with the constant state of change this life entails, God is always with us. God is love. Think about that feeling of being in love which is the greatest feeling in the world. God created that for us.

Think About It:
What are the things that make you happy?

What Makes You Happy?

Experiencing happiness is an individualized experience. You see it all the time. You go to a social event and one person had the time of their life while another was bored to tears. It all depended on how they interpreted the event. Some people liked the music, others did not. Some connected with the guests while others did not. It was the same event but the people who experienced it were different.

Introverts feel happy when they are with a small group of friends or even just having time to themselves. Extroverts feel happy when they are the center of attention and thrive within large groups of people. Which are you? Knowing who you are and what you want out of life will allow you to find your happiness.

Imagine buying a friend a birthday present. If they are a close friend, you will want to put some thought into it. You need to know what your friend wants or at least what interests they have in order to find a gift they will appreciate. I'm sure you would not think twice about putting in this time for the benefit of your friend. If you would put effort into the gift-buying process for a friend, why would you not put the same kind of energy into getting to know yourself and your own interests?

I love this scripture from the book of Psalms. It acknowledges that God wants us to be happy. "Trust in the Lord instead. Be kind and good to others; then you will live safely here in the land and prosper, feeding in safety. Be delighted with the Lord. Then he will give you all your heart's desires." (Psalm 37:3-4 TLB) We can pursue our own happiness without being hedonistic. God wants us to be good to others. He also wants to be good to us and provide us with our desires. My question to you, however, is "Do you know what you want?" This may sound silly, but you would be surprised at how many people do not know what they really want. Of course, we all want to be rich and thin and have someone to love us. But how much money do you really need? Money may not be the most important thing in this world but when you don't have it, then it sure becomes important. How thin do you want to be? Or is it a particular look you are going for? What lifestyle can you withstand to maintain this look? Yes, everyone would like to eat whatever they want and be thin, but this is not reality. There are no magic wands. If you want to find the perfect mate, have you asked yourself what qualities you want them to possess? Do you know what you are looking for?

Are you living based on your own priorities, or what you think you should be doing? According to Alicia Menendez in her book *The Likeability Trap* "If one's major life choices are dictated entirely by what one should do, what is expected, rather than what is authentic to oneself, it would seem impossible to live a happy, self-actualized life." To simplify this, are you being true to yourself?

Still need a little help? Look at the following areas of your life to provide you with some balance. You may not want to set goals in each area but remember this is just a guide. Here is the list, in no particular order:

1. Spirituality
2. Health & Appearance

3. Finances
4. Relationships (family, friends, romantic)
5. Career
6. Hobbies/Interests (includes travel)
7. Living Environment & Possessions
8. Bucket List

1. **Spirituality** – This book is written from a Christian perspective. Maybe you may have spiritual goals of getting baptized, going on a mission trip, tithing or finally becoming a member of the church you have been attending. How about serving at that church? Do you want to start a Christian non-profit agency, write a Christian book, read the Bible in its entirety, write a Christian song, perform in a Christian band, or maybe attend a Christian conference?

2. **Health & Appearance** – This would include areas such as losing weight, building muscle, running a 10k, lowering your A1C, starting a skincare routine, taking care of dental health, and committing to a regular pattern of sleep, just for a few examples. Health is also an important area because, without our health, we lose many opportunities in life. Our body is a temple, and we must show respect for it. I know that is easier said than done. It is a daily task but one you will not regret. Most older people, when asked to advise their younger self, will state they wished they had taken better care of their bodies.

3. **Finances** – Goals here could include opening an IRA, making consistent contributions to a savings account, paying off debt, and earning 10 percent more than the previous year. This is an area where we need to consider our long-term goals. Without

money, many areas of life are limited. Even our health could be compromised if we cannot afford adequate medical care.

4. **Relationships (family, friends, romantic)** – Items here could involve having more children, taking care of elderly parents, maintaining date nights with your spouse, bonding with your children through family time, spending quality time with friends, and keeping in touch with those you do not see often. If you are single, you may want to date and increase your social network.

5. **Career** – These goals could involve changing careers, increasing your education, enhancing your knowledge in your current career, mentoring a new colleague, attending a conference in your field, increasing productivity at work, the list can go on and on and I'm sure your supervisor will have lots of additional ideas for you. Perhaps you have an entrepreneurial spirit and want to be the one in charge by starting your own business.

6. **Hobbies/Interests (includes travel)** – These goals can include: increasing social activities, attending sporting events and concerts, traveling, or learning a new sport. This may also include intellectual pursuits such as learning a new language, completing that list of books you want to read, and starting a blog or podcast. Just please don't tell me you want to increase your social media followers! (If you do, then I hope it is for business purposes.)

7. **Living Environment & Possessions** – This area involves items such as the kind of home you want, type of vehicle, home furnishings, perhaps work you want to be done to your home, or obtaining items related to your hobbies, etc.

8. **Bucket List –** This is the area where you get permission to go a little crazy. In Section II, we will talk about The Bucket List and how to create one. When you think about your wants in life, don't forget to break the mold and do something different.

These areas can easily blend into each other. The point is to get an idea of what you want to accomplish to add enjoyment and meaning to your life. The possibilities are endless. When you sit down to list your desires, the first ones are the most obvious because they are on the front of your mind. They may even be items you have seen accomplished by friends. Keep a running list. Once you cross off one goal from your list, add another to replace it. As you go through life, various possibilities will present themselves to you. During a time of self-reflection, rate yourself in terms of your current happiness. Are you pleased with the direction your life is headed? Are you happy or merely content? Do you want to continue living the same lifestyle ten years from now?

How Do You Know When You Are Happy?

Being happy with your life does not mean everything is perfect and running smoothly. Throughout our lives, we go through many seasons. There will always be troubled times, or "winters" as many refer to it, which we must deal with. Often it is going through the winters that makes you appreciate the "summers" much beter. Happiness takes work. Anyone can complain. It's easy and does not require much thought. State three things about an event you attended that you did not like. Listing the negatives is easy, but now state three positives about that event. Focusing on the positive aspects may require some insight and higher-level thought.

> Being happy with your life does not mean everything is perfect and running smoothly.

It's time to get serious and realistic about what we really want in our lives. For most people, it is around the end of the year when they look over their lives to determine what they want. Personally, I find birthdays to be a time of self-reflection, yet I know adults who chose not to celebrate their own birthday. Most people rely on television and social media as a reminder to reflect upon their past year and help them decide on setting New Year's resolutions. Do you still make New Year's resolutions? I have heard it said that most New Year's resolutions do not make it through the month of February. Creating one's goals is not a fad and should not be dictated by commentaries made during Dick Clark's New Year's Rockin' Eve special.

Do You Know What You Want?

Do you know what you want out of life? Do you know what you want right now? If so, can you describe it? For this to be done you should sit quietly, with no distractions, a clean sheet of paper and writing instrument. If you need to, set a timer for ten minutes. Write down all the things you want. You may think you have done this after a minute or two but keep going. If you cannot think of any more then sit for the remainder of the time and just think. Remember, no interruptions allowed. Usually, you need this time because other goals will slowly enter your mind. Once the ten minutes are up, think about these desires and divide them into both long and short-term goals. Project one year, five years and then long-term into the future. Most of the time, long-term will be about ten years into the future but it depends upon your age range. Younger people may project further into the future while older folks may consider ten years as far out as they would like to go. You may consider some of your desires too outlandish to even document because there is no way they could become a reality, at least not in your life. Do not limit yourself. Let's look at what we are told in the book of Proverbs, "Trust in the Lord with all your heart; do not depend on your own understanding. Seek his will in all you do, and he will show you which path to take." (Proverbs 3:5-6 NLT) If we went through this world only depending on our own understanding we would not accomplish very much. Think of all the lessons you learned in school. All the information your father and grandfather taught you. Have you ever been stumped by a problem and sought guidance through an online video or reference manual? This all demonstrates how you seek out understanding, not just from your own brain but from others. If you seek information and understanding from other people, then why not from God? Who can we trust more than our Heavenly Father? God will show us the direction to take but you must first seek Him out. Talk with Him. Tell Him what concerns you have, problems you need to work on, or dreams you are trying to make a reality. You are probably thinking God already knows this, He knows what is in our hearts. You are right, but going to God with these concerns is an integral part of making an investment in our personal relationship with Him. Have you ever gone to your parents to discuss an issue only to discover that they were already aware of the situation? It's the same thing. They were just waiting for you to come to them. Many parents would even report feeling hurt that they were not sought out for advice earlier. How do you think God feels? Remember, we were created in His image.

Once you have sought God out, you must be attentive to listen for His response. This is where most people will drop out of the process. Because He is our Heavenly Father, His voice will not be as clear to our ears in the same manner as when you call your brother-in-law on the phone and ask for his advice. God does, however, speak through other people, dreams, and as that little voice inside of us. The problem is we may not recognize it immediately. Some people may want something so desperately that they look for anything as a "sign". When you are open and want to hear from God you must make time for Him. Be quiet, allow no distractions, and listen. You also may choose to listen for God when playing worship music.

Journaling to God can also be helpful. Write out ways in which you appreciate His blessings. Write out your requests to Him, then when He answers these requests, document it. Trust in God. He has plans for our lives. He will guide us on the route to take. No dream is too large for our God.

Clarity

As we get further into this book, you will notice the importance of having a clear vision of what you want. Picture a grocery shopping trip. Think of when you have gone to the store with a list. You know what meals you want to make and have a list of the items you will need to create those meals. You shop according to your list. There may be a few items unavailable, so you may have to make adjustments. Now remember the times you have gone grocery shopping without making a list. You grab whatever seems appealing at the time. You probably buy way too much junk food and find yourself holding a large grocery receipt while stating "There is nothing to eat in this house!" This analogy applies to our wants in life. We have an idea of what makes us happy, but we need to be clear about it. Sure, we can go to the grocery store to see if there is something good, and occasionally something does hit the spot for us. Is this the way you want to go through life, with your attainment of dreams, just waiting for an opportunity to jump out at you? If I asked you what you want for dinner you might say "Something good", perhaps you would be more specific and state "Italian". Ideally, you would be clear and state "I want that Fettuccini dish like we had last week". The more specific you are, the more likely you will get what you are asking for.

Keeping It Simple

According to Abraham Maslow's Hierarchy of Needs, we need to take care of our basic needs for food, shelter, and a sense of safety before we can reach the higher aspirations of self-actualization. This does not mean someone homeless cannot feel happiness, love, or gratitude. To be realistic, however, no one wants to live a life of constant struggle. I think as Christians, we can all agree that it feels much better to be the one giving than having to be the recipient. If we do find that we are on the receiving end of gifts, we can certainly show appreciation and learn to pass it forward.

If I had to simplify it, I would say the keys to happiness involve being content in four areas of your life: God, health, love, and finances. This is not to suggest that if you are lacking in these areas, you cannot feel joy. These areas, however, are core to fulfillment in life.

God – Our relationship with the Lord is the most important relationship we have. Throughout our lives, loved ones will come and go but the Lord will always be with us. This is a relationship we should never take for granted.

Health – In our physical life we need good health. Without our health what do we have? We cannot outsource our health. No one can do that workout for you, no one can take that blood test or lower that cholesterol but you. We need our health to enjoy our lives. No one wants to live a life with physical pain or limitations. Take care of your health, eat right, exercise, and don't forget to make those medical checkups a priority. Try not to let work obligations interfere with this. Taking care of small health issues before they grow can save your life.

Love – Having love in our lives is the icing on top of the cake. The love we feel for others often gets us through the tough times. It often gives us a reason to survive. Then, of course, there is romantic love which truly is a gift from God. Make sure your loved ones know that you love and appreciate them.

Finances – Perhaps it sounds shallow, but money is important. Money may not buy happiness, however, when you lack funds, it can create a great deal of stress. The best advice in terms of finances is to not just live within your means but below it. Try to live in the 10-10-80 zone. Most financial experts agree that the first ten percent of your income should be to charity, as a Christian this would be your tithe to God. The next ten percent of your income should go to your savings account. This will allow you funds to rely on in case of emergencies. This leaves you with the remaining eighty percent of your income on which to live.

Opportunities and Prayer

There are times when opportunities will present themselves to us and it is wonderful when we can take advantage of these events. The reality, however, is that to fulfill our dreams, we must create our own opportunities. Right about now, I can hear you thinking "If it is meant to be then God will make it happen". Yes, that is true, but God wants us to play our part. If it was meant for you to earn an A in math class, then do you even need to study? I know I would! Through prayer and a plan, you can make the majority of your dreams come to fruition. Let's look at (John 16:24 NLT) "You haven't done this before. Ask, using my name, and you will receive, and you will have abundant joy." Do you ask God to have your wants met? Why not? Are you afraid to bother Him? Our God is limitless. There is no end to the blessings He can bestow upon us. Does it feel selfish to pray for your wants? There is war, famine, and abuse in the world, and you feel that asking for a better income is greedy. I get it. It is normal to want to pray for ourselves. If you feel greedy then perhaps that is your conscious telling you to look out for the needs of others. Helping others is a wonderful feeling. Putting a focus on other people helps us to put our grievances into perspective. When we receive blessings, we can share them. We can ask for a larger income, but we should also tithe from that income. Are your wants something that can also benefit others? Do not hoard your blessings. Allow your good fortunes to also bless others.

Your Turn:

In each of the eight areas list at least one thing you desire. Put an asterisk by the top three that resonate with you.

1. Spirituality–

2. Health & Appearance–

3. Finances–

4. Relationships–

5. Career–

6. Hobbies/Interests -

7. Living Environment & Possessions-

8. Bucket List-

"If you don't know who you truly are, you'll never know what you really want."

- Roy T. Bennett

Chapter 2

Snapshots of Life: Understanding the Life Cycle

This is the chapter I most looked forward to writing. It is about the stages we go through during life. It is about reflection as well as looking forward. If someone were to take a brief view of your life today, what would it reveal? Would the manner in which you are portraying your life today be an accurate appraisal of who you are, or would you be saying "They just have to get to know me?" Who we are today is not only a result of our personality but also our life choices and the experiences we have undergone.

My Snapshot

A thought that comes to mind regarding snapshots, is one involving an encounter I had with an old high school friend. I was close with this person through high school, then college, as well as after college when we started our careers. As I'm sure you can guess, once she got married and I moved out of state we lost touch. Now, I am dating myself here, but this was in a time before internet use. Time marched on and then there was social media. Of course, I was not one of the first to join these websites. I feared these sites may be scams! So, by the time I joined, most of my school chums were already established with their online profiles. Once I set up my profile, I was pleased to have old friends, many of whom I had not been in touch with for over twenty years, send contact requests. My old friend was one of them. After accepting her request, she sent a private message telling me how happy she was to be back in touch with me. I also agreed that it was great to be in contact with her once again. She then sent me a message updating me on her life since there were many "missing episodes". Her message went something like this:

Still fat, still married, still working, at same old job, bought a townhouse, still living in the area, no kids.

Wow, she summed up almost ten years in one sentence! She asked how I was doing, and I responded using the same format:

Still fat, still married, making a career change, bought a house, still in Texas, doing foster care.

It reminds me of how people respond when the time comes around for a high school or college reunion. We suddenly stop and take a snapshot of our life. We reflect upon our hopes and dreams from back in our school days and assess whether we have stayed on track.

Train Wreck

Life definitely has a way of derailing us. Health issues, financial problems, family emergencies, none of us are immune. Usually, people experience some sort of crisis event a few times a year. This may be your own crisis or one of a friend/family member. Sometimes this event is major such as a health crisis or death in the family, and sometimes it is inconvenient such as a rise in household bills requiring a re-negotiation of one's financial budget. The point is that we must expect the ups and downs in life and be prepared to roll with it. The ability to be flexible is a desirable trait. "...while the earth remains, seedtime and harvest, cold and heat, summer and winter, day and night, shall not cease." (Genesis 8:22 ESV) Just as the earth has seasons, so does our life. There will be problems in our lives that are unavoidable but there are also times when the problems are resolved.

> We must expect the ups and downs in life and be prepared to roll with it.

Maybe you feel your peers are further along in life than you are. That can definitely feel discouraging, especially in this age of social media, where it seems that people's accomplishments are just thrown in your face. I can't really say that I blame them. It feels good to share your accomplishments with others and see those likes, or thumbs up, in the corner of your posts. When people share their highlights, be happy for them. Your time will come. There is a time for everything in our life. "A time to love and a time to hate, a time for war and a time for peace." (Ecclesiastes 3:8 NIV) This scripture tells me that it is okay to acknowledge our disappointments and regrets as long as we don't stay there and wallow in it. Each phase of life has a season. If you are in a discouraging season, use that time to celebrate others in their joyous events. There is a time for you to shine and a time to allow others to shine. Be present for the people in your life by nurturing the relationship in both the trying times and the celebratory times.

The Life Snapshot

Back to our life snapshot; because we were in our mid-adult age, the list my friend and I exchanged was appropriate. If we were in our late teens or early twenties it may have looked something like this:

Still living at home (getting ready to move out), got a car, two more semesters till graduation, new boyfriend, still working my part-time job.

Depending on what stage of life you are in, there are specific tasks or life events that you want to reach. For a recent high school graduate, items such as where and with whom they are living, education, a vehicle, employment, friends and social life are a priority. By mid-adulthood, the items change from where one is living to what house one has purchased, a vehicle is naturally assumed, employment may focus on higher level education and training, salary, and amount of prestige one has in their career. Friendships and social life, although they still may be present, are exchanged for a focus on one's spouse and children.

Notice the three commonalities: Residence, Career, and Relationships. I also feel it is important to add a fourth commonality that may not be directly stated but it is there, that of physical appearance.

Residence—For a child, one's residence may include items such as whether they live in a house or an apartment, who lives in their home such as extended family members, as well as if the residence is stable such as with families who must move around for various reasons. For young adults, a major milestone is the entire issue of moving out of the family home. Living in a dorm and sharing an apartment with friends are significant life events. As one grows older and matures, home ownership is usually a goal. Living in a particular area of the country or perhaps even abroad may be the focus of one's efforts. In later years, this switches to whether one's children or perhaps even their own parents live at home with them as many people are caring for their aging family. In the final stages of life, residence is also an issue in terms of living independently at home or having family members live with them so they can receive care. Options such as assisted living and retirement homes are also considerations for one's residence at this stage of life.

Career—Employment is an area of one's life that can take many different forms. For a child, attending school is their career. After high school, it may be college with the focus on a major or attending a technical/trade school. This may or may not involve working an actual job during these years.

Perhaps the military is a career of choice. Homemaking may also be a career of focus even though the media does not give it the credibility for which it rightly deserves. In youth, getting those entry-level jobs is exciting. As we age, it is anticipated we earn our credentials and make strides in our careers. Many of us may even start our own businesses. As one ages, the issue of retirement may be a focus. Many people have detailed strategies for the building of their retirement accounts.

Relationships – Because we do not live in a bubble, relationships will always be a consideration. Even if you are a loner, you will still need to maintain some sort of relationship, even if it is only with your internet provider! (Just kidding.) A social life, or lack of one, is often a source of either joy or despair. People vary in their social interactions, some have friends, some have family only and some have a combination. As we are growing up, we must have relationships with our parents and siblings, referred to as our family of orientation. Remember when you were a teenager and denied that you even had parents? Our focus later will be on dating and obtaining a spouse. Then there is our relationship with our children. This family, our spouse and children, are referred to as our family of procreation. As we go through life, our focus from family of orientation often transfers to focusing on our family of procreation and then back to our family of orientation as our parents age. We go from the roles of child to spouse to parent to grandparent and perhaps, even great grandparent. Along this journey with our family, we make friends. Some of these friendships may be created with bonds stronger than those you even have with family members.

Physical Appearance – This is the area that some people may not acknowledge to others, but it is there. Whether we admit to it or not, we judge people's appearance. Maybe it is that we notice how our once strong-looking father is now frail. Maybe, we see the signs of stress on our best friend's face in the form of wrinkles. For many of us, we look at old pictures and see how our youth has faded away. This is what many people fear during a high school reunion, the thought that we do not look as youthful and attractive as we did "back in the day". Have you ever looked at an old picture of yourself and remembered how horrible you thought you looked at the time? Now, years later, you wish you were looking like that! As we age, we may find we become more accepting of the imperfections associated with our personal appearance. We finally find ourselves becoming comfortable in our own skin. In my example at the beginning of this chapter, it is her looks that my high school friend mentioned first when giving me the snapshot of her life when she reported: "still fat". Think about your social media profiles, they have a picture attached to them. It always makes me suspicious of how a person feels about themselves when the profile picture is of their pet rather than themself. This is not to suggest that something is wrong, it is just the first impression it makes upon me.

The Retirement Party

How would you like people to describe you during your retirement party? I could have just as easily asked how you wanted to be talked about at your funeral, but that is a little morbid. Besides, as many will say, you won't be around to hear it. What about your legacy? How do you want to be remembered? At your retirement party, you will get to listen to the good things people say, as well as judge whether or not they are embellishing. It also allows you the opportunity to turn things around if you feel necessary.

> **Think About it:**
> **What do you want people to say about you at your retirement?**

Psychosocial Development

Having a degree in social work, I have taken many human development courses and studied many theorists. One of my favorites was Erik Erikson and his Theory of Psychosocial Development. According to Erikson, at each stage of our lives, we have tasks we are working on that we should accomplish. Erikson's Stages of Psychosocial Development range from age birth through old age. Notice the term being used is psycho-social. Psych refers to the individual and their mental functioning and social refers to interaction with others. In the book *The Life Cycle Completed,* Erikson reports "An individual life cycle cannot be adequately understood apart from the social context in which it comes to fruition. Individual and society are intricately woven, dynamically interrelated in continual exchange." We do not live in a bubble therefore when we have goals we are working toward, the people in our lives will influence it. Sometimes our relationships help to propel us forward and sometimes they hold us back. Relationships are a part of our existence that we cannot ignore. We influence other people whether we realize it or not. Thanks to cell phones, social media, and surveillance systems, our actions are being viewed now more than at any other time in history. How are you presenting yourself? Would people view you as someone going someplace in life? Would they recognize you as a follower of Christ?

The following represents the psychosocial stages discussed by Erikson. It is listed by age, basic conflict for that stage, along with the virtue to hopefully be attained. This is to give you a general idea. I am not an expert on Erikson's Psychosocial Developmental Stages, but I present them here so that if you are so inclined you may conduct further research.

Age	Basic Conflict	Virtue
Birth–18 mos	Trust vs Mistrust	Hope
2–3	Autonomy vs Shame & Doubt	Will
3–5	Initiative vs Guilt	Purpose
6–11	Industry vs Inferiority	Competence
12–18	Identity vs Identity Confusion	Fidelity
19–40	Intimacy vs Isolation	Love
40–65	Generativity vs Stagnation	Care
65+	Integrity vs Despair	Wisdom

For now, I will give you my synopsis, in very general terms regarding these stages. Think about your childhood and trying to do things by yourself. Exploring and making friends outside of your family. Now think about your teen years, a time when acceptance is crucial. Our friendships become closer with more trust built between and among our peers. It is a time of establishing our identity. Our individuality is being explored and is often influenced by society. During young adulthood, the crisis being addressed is intimacy versus isolation. Romantic relationships are being negotiated. In older adulthood (ages forty to sixty-five), the crisis is generativity versus stagnation. A focus on career and ensuring that one's life is making a difference. Thoughts are turning to leaving a legacy. The eighth stage is age sixty-five and older and focuses on integrity versus despair. This is the stage in which one questions one's life choices. Regrets are focused on. In his book, Erikson reports adding on a ninth stage to this life cycle. He reports "It is useful to delineate a specific time frame in order to focus on the life experiences and crises of the period. Old age in one's eighties and nineties brings with it new demands, reevaluations, and daily difficulties." Obviously, we begin our lives by being dependent on others to take care of us, and then toward the end of our lives (if we are privileged enough to live this long) by being dependent on others again.

What Do These Psychosocial Stages Mean to You?

Have you identified the stage of life you are in? Does it matter? Yes, it does. Acknowledging the stage you are in helps you to make short-term goals for your immediate future as well as long-term goals. It also helps to look at your loved ones and the stage they are in. Perhaps you are worried about your daughter. Knowing what stage she is in as well as what psychosocial issues she is dealing with can help you to help her, or at least understand where she is coming from. Or maybe you feel that your son is acting out. In looking at these stages you may realize that he is going through issues related to his psychosocial stage. This knowledge may help ease worry about the situation. Please keep in mind that these are merely guidelines. Obviously, we all have unique personalities so as the saying goes, "Results may vary".

Self-Evaluation

Self-evaluation will occur at different times for different people. For instance, class reunions don't come around every year. When they do, I end up comparing myself to others my age. We graduated at the same time, went to the same school, lived in the same geographical area, and pretty much had the same background. Given all the similarities, it is no wonder people played the comparison game during this time. Sure, it can make you feel bad if you do not think you are at the same level as your peers. We can also choose to reframe the situation; by seeing where your peers are, you are given role models to guide your progress. If you find yourself feeling discouraged, remind yourself of this quote by President Theodore Roosevelt: "...comparison is the thief of joy."

Personally, birthdays have always been a time of reflection for me. As each year passes, I look at where I am in life and ponder if I like where I am, where I came from, and where I am headed. I take assessments of the positive choices I have made and congratulate myself on them. I also look at poor choices, or missed opportunities, and acknowledge them for what they are. I review areas where not making a decision was in fact, over time, actually making a decision. I have learned to forgive myself for certain choices as I know I am human and therefore flawed. I try to remind myself that what is truly in God's plan will come to fruition, regardless of how off-track I find myself. I realize some people have larger regrets than others. I suggest, that if there is an area in your life you truly cannot let go of, which is holding you back, you should seek out counseling. Several sessions of counseling really could provide the clarity needed in one's life to help ease the process of moving forward.

> Not making a decision was in fact, over time, actually making a decision.

"Have I not commanded you? Be strong and courageous. Do not be afraid; do not be discouraged, for the LORD your God will be with you wherever you go." (Joshua 1:9 NIV) I love that we are being told not to be discouraged. The Lord knows that we do get discouraged in this life, and there are times when we feel like giving up, but we can't hide it from God. He already knows our hearts. God will get us back on the right track!

Snapshots of Life:Understanding the Life Cycle

Your Turn:

Write out the snapshot of your life today.

Date:_____

List 3 things you like about this.

1. _____
2. _____
3. _____

List 3 things you would change.

1. _____
2. _____
3. _____

"Life is like riding a bicycle, to keep your balance, you must keep moving."

-Albert Einstein

Chapter 3

Your Past: Perspectives Influencing Your Future

Do you wear sneakers? If so, how long are your shoelaces? Have you ever tripped over those shoelaces because of their length? Sometimes in life, our emotional shoestrings are too long. We find ourselves getting hung up because of our past. There are some experiences in life we may wish to forget. Ahh, how a good dose of amnesia would be nice! Every action we take is based on our past experiences. Knowing who you are now, as well as where you have come from, is crucial to getting you to that ideal destination in your future. Most of the time, we respond in a predictable manner. Our actions are consistent with our personality. Who we are today is a result of our life experiences.

Our core is what remains constant with us through the years. For instance, have you ever asked yourself "What would _____ do?" and correctly identified the type of advice this loved one would give you? It is because you know their core. But as we go through life, things happen that change us. Are you using these experiences to make you a better person or to become jaded? After all, no one gets through this life without having experienced joys as well as sorrows.

How You Were Wronged

Why is it that we always seem to remember the bad before the good? Unfortunately, negative experiences are a part of life. Why do some people hang onto these experiences while others can move forward or use it as leverage to succeed?

Some people go into denial and repress their bad experiences. Denial can be tricky, as it is not always a bad thing. Denial is a mechanism used by our minds to protect us from something we may not be able to emotionally handle. Denial should be temporary, just for a season. Eventually, our issues must be dealt with otherwise we will find ourselves stuck. How well you deal with a negative incident will depend on the severity of the experience and/or the season of life you were in when the event occurred. Knowing that negative encounters are an unfortunate part of life should help us reframe these episodes to make them growth opportunities. Unfortunately, we cannot choose when these bad experiences will occur or what they will be.

Whether you suffered abuse, were swindled out of your life savings, or had your heart broken, we have all been hurt by other people. There is now an element of broken trust which we had in others. Many times, that lack of trust gets transferred onto other people, good people, in our lives. In some cases, there may be an element of regret "Why did I allow _____ to happen?" In order to live our life to the fullest, we must move on from this. To move forward we must acknowledge the pain or loss we experienced. Ignoring it may help temporarily but then that pain will eventually resurface. Some experiences in life will profoundly change us and we cannot return to who we were. Life is not fair, and no one promised that it would be. Suffering an injury in an accident or health issues may alter your way of life. Once you acknowledge that change, which can be a long process for some, only then you can move on to your "new normal". Your life may not look the way you want it to, but instead of using your energy to lament upon what might have been, you must move forward. Use your pain as a vehicle for transformation. Life is short. We cannot afford to waste it in any way. Try to use the negative experiences to help others.

> To move forward we must acknowledge the pain or loss we experienced.

When it comes to emotional pain, we must employ the adage that "The best revenge is living well". Learning to trust again can be difficult. There is no guarantee that we will not be taken advantage of again. It becomes quite paradoxical that the more we protect ourselves, the more we get in our way. Learning to identify warning signs is imperative. Once those red flags are identified we must follow our instincts and learn how to protect ourselves. This process takes practice. In the case of abuse,

I suggest seeking out professional counseling. Some people get hooked upon the stigma associated with seeking out this kind of help. They do not want to go to a "shrink". There are many different types of counselors out there to choose from. There are Licensed Professional Counselors (LPCs), Licensed Clinical Social Workers (LCSWs), Licensed Marriage and Family Therapists (LMFTs), psychologists (PhDs & PsyDs) as well as Christian counselors. Each counseling professional has their own specialty and therapy style. It does not mean you need to spend the rest of your life in therapy. You may only need a few sessions or to go for a season in your life. If you have a history of abuse, mental health issues, or addictions you are having difficulty resolving on your own, you owe it to yourself to seek out a professional counselor. This would fall under the category of self-care.

> **Think About it:**
> **Is there anything from your past that you are clinging on to that is currently holding you back?**

Reflect on issues from your past. Is there anything you are clinging to that is holding you back from moving forward in your life? If there is, then I want to ask you this "What purpose is holding onto it currently serving you?" Many people hold on to anger and bitterness from areas in their lives in which they feel wronged. How does this anger serve them? Some may say that they use this as a barrier so that they will not be hurt or taken advantage of again. In Ephesians, we are told to "Get rid of all bitterness, rage and anger, brawling and slander, along with every form of malice. Be kind and compassionate to one another, forgiving each other, just as in Christ God forgave you." (Ephesians 4:31-32 NIV) This scripture acknowledges that we will experience feelings of anger and bitterness. Getting over anger is so much easier said than done. Anger is a normal human emotion, and it is okay to feel it. Anger is hurt turned inside out. To put it another way, anger and hurt are different sides of the same coin. Acknowledge your angered feelings. Use those feelings to fuel actions that have a positive impact then let it go. The bitterness from anger serves no purpose but to damage your future. We need to learn from our experiences and move forward. Forgiveness is also ordered with a reminder of how Christ has forgiven us.

Some people just seem to have it all: looks, talent, money. They seem to get all the breaks. You may ask "Why can't I have all that?" Or maybe you were dealt a bad hand; unable to have children, parents dying early, physical illness, being a victim of a natural disaster, the list can go on and on. The important thing to remember is not to compare ourselves to others. When we compare ourselves to others we will lose every time. Remember, these perfect people may only be perfect in how they mask their issues. No one has the perfect life. What you see on the outside or on social media is often a person's highlight reel and not necessarily a reflection of one's everyday activities. Thanks to social media, many of us experience FOMO (fear of missing out). We fear others are having an exciting life without us. Although I realize this can be an anxious feeling, please do not give in to it. If we make any kind of comparisons, it should be to compare your current self to your prior self.

Self-Sabotage

Most people are their own worst enemy. We end up self-sabotaging when we don't let go of our past. The only thing we can count on in life is change. No matter how much we desire to remain at a certain stage in life, we cannot. Life moves on whether we want it to or not. At a certain point, you must accept this. Would you really want to stay at the same place in life while your peers were moving on? You may have regrets that you continue to blame yourself for. You long for a "do-over" but our lives do not allow a rewind. Learn to forgive yourself. Many times, we forgive others but forget to give the same grace to ourselves. We must move forward. Moving forward is for the best. If we spent our entire lives focusing on the past, we would not be able to enjoy the new things the Lord is bringing to us. Use these experiences as learning opportunities. Learn from your mistakes as you move on. If it is in God's plan, then He will bring new opportunities to you. Many times, these opportunities brought by the Lord are even better than what you may have desired.

> We end up self-sabotaging when we don't let go of our past.

Your Glory Days

How was your youth? Do you look upon it with a smile on your face? Do you reminisce about it with old friends? Do you tell new friends stories about "back in the day"? It is a beautiful thing if you have a past that you can smile about. Many people are not so fortunate. Reliving the past can cheer us up when we are feeling down. It can even be a coping skill to open the old vault and pull out those memories. During our elder years, we have our memories and the knowledge of people our lives impacted. I am a sentimental and nostalgic person so I can appreciate the joy people have when reliving those memories of their glory days. However, we must put it in perspective. There is nothing more pitiful than when old friends gather and only spend their time reliving the past. Then what do they do—reminisce about the reminiscing? Try not to fall into that trap. There is a quote from Roy T. Bennett that sums up the perspective one should use regarding their past: "The past is a place of reference, not a place of residence;..." This quote acknowledges the importance of our past but reminds us that what lies in front of us should be the primary focus of our attention and where we need to put our effort.

"Forget the former things; do not dwell on the past. See I am doing a new thing! Now it springs up; do you not perceive it? I am making a way in the wilderness and streams in the wasteland." (Isaiah 43:18-19 NIV) This is a scripture about not dwelling on the past. Our memories make us who we are but there are times when we need to emotionally let go. Make it a point to make new memories. Many people love to reflect on those times when they were in their prime. It is often said that "Youth is wasted on the young". It can make us feel sad that we will never be in our prime again. The It's all downhill from here" mentality can be depressing. Life goes on and so we must move on as well. The past can be bittersweet; we can look back and smile yet feel melancholy that it is in our rearview mirror. Just keep moving on because there are new joys, not necessarily the same kind, but there will be joy. As we age, certain options may disappear and then we must seek new opportunities. These opportunities are out there but as we age, we must search more diligently for them.

Recent Successes

Have you been doing well recently? Are you proud of yourself? It's great to feel confident in something you have accomplished. But just as we cannot live in our failures, we also cannot bask in our glories for too long. As you learn how to create bucket lists, vision boards, and set goals, you will discover that once you reach one goal then it will be time to set another. Part of the reason some people feel incomplete is that they are spending their time trying to please others. The only one we should be striving to please is the Lord. Acknowledge the fact that as we go through life, experiencing both the good and bad as well as encountering various people, our expectations of what we want out of life will change. "So, get rid of your old self, which made you live as you used to—the old self that was being destroyed by its deceitful desires. Your hearts and minds must be made completely new, and you must put on the new self, which is created in God's likeness and reveals itself in the true life that is upright and holy." (Ephesians 4:22-24 GNT) This scripture acknowledges the changes we go through in life. It is okay to leave parts of ourselves behind. Hopefully as you go through life you are growing and maturing as a person. Now I am not saying to let go of everything. There are many accomplishments in your life for which you should be proud. There are accomplishments you achieved that are building blocks for you to move forward in life and that is great. If they are working for you now, then keep them. If, however, something stops working for you, do not continue it merely because it worked for you many years ago.

Journaling

As a writer, I am a big proponent of journaling. Journaling is a great way to get those feelings out of your head. There will be times when venting to others can be helpful and then there will be times when venting to yourself is more productive. Journaling is part of venting to yourself. It is an emotional outlet, a catharsis. When you journal, it is for your eyes only. You can feel free to write how you are truly feeling without having to censor yourself for fear of offending others. Think of your journal as a safe space. You will have the experience of both writing in your journal and then reading back what you have written. A journal entry also serves as a record of your progress. You can go back over your journals as the months pass and determine how you were feeling back then compared to now. Journaling fosters a sense of self-awareness. Keeping a journal will allow you to gain insight into your emotional reactions as well as their triggers. It can also allow you to view any behavioral patterns you may be displaying. You can monitor growth. "Wow, I can't believe how emotional I was back then." You may take a look from a different perspective and realize that you have been hanging on to certain issues for too long. It is perfectly normal to hang onto some emotions, after all you are human, but when these emotions interfere with your progression in life then it is a problem. Journaling can be a way of acknowledging those crippling emotions so that you can deal with them.

Do you know how to journal? Well, guess what? It is not as difficult as it may seem. There really is no wrong way to journal. It is, however, most helpful to date your entries. This will aid you when attempting to review your progress at a later time. Most people write in their journals while others use bullet points to document their feelings. Some write poetry to express feelings and others may put it in the form of a prayer. Some people who dislike writing may want to use illustrations such as a broken heart or a happy face. If this is how you express yourself then go ahead and do it, but please also try to put a label to your illustration. Part of self-awareness is being able to identify the specific feelings you are having. It is important to acknowledge the severity of your feelings. Does that emoji you just drew mean that you were angry, irritated, frustrated, or infuriated?

It is helpful to journal daily, much like writing in a diary. There will be days, no matter how much you may enjoy this journaling, that you do not write. It is those missing days that also provide data for your emotional journey. You may review your journal from three months earlier and wonder why there were several missing days. Perhaps those were days when so much was going on that you had no time for journaling. Maybe you recognize a pattern that you journal daily and now you only journal a few times a week. This may indicate that you are getting over an emotional pain and that the intensity of the emotion is being reduced.

1. Date the entry.
2. Journal using your own style.
3. Label feelings as well as their intensity.
4. Review your entries from time to time.

Your past has an impact on your present reactions and choices. These current choices will influence your future. Enjoy your pleasant memories and learn from those heartbreaking experiences. Identify where there are cycles that need to change. When you identify a cycle that needs to be broken, act on it immediately. Do not waste your precious life. If you do not act on it now, then when?

Your Turn:

List five things you are proud of about your life: (do not stop until you have at least five).

1. _____

2. _____

3. _____

4. _____

5. _____

List five regrets you have in life (if you do not have five that is okay).

1. _____

2. _____

3. _____

4. _____

5. _____

Write one thing you could let go of in order to move forward in life:

Section II

Dreams and Making Them a Reality

In the first section of this book, you explored who you are and what you wanted out of life. You even had an opportunity to engage in some dreaming. Now it is time to make a plan for fulfilling these dreams. Life is short so we need to embrace it! Take control of your life and follow through with these plans. Prince Charming is not going to show up and whisk you off your feet. You don't need to wait for him. You can start working on your dreams today!

In Section II, we are going to discuss the fun process of creating a bucket list, a vision board as well as how to set measurable goals. Make sure you have paper and a pen ready as you work your way through this section.

Dear Lord,

I'm praying you show me the goals you want me to fulfill this year. Please help me to live a life that is within your will. Help me to honor you in my heart and through my actions. Guide me as I create my plan for the year by setting these goals and creating my vision board. Allow me to keep my focus on you far above everything and to use my success as a vehicle to show worship and praise to you.

Amen

"The yearly Bucket List Oath

I solemnly swear to create memories that last a lifetime. I vow to make an impression on the world, not the couch. I promise to dream about unrealistic goals, and make them my reality."

- Unknown

Chapter 4

The Bucket List: Adding Sprinkles to Your Life

Excitement! Adventure! Death? Limited time? Last chance? How about silliness? When I say the term bucket list what comes to your mind? For most people, when they hear the term bucket list they think of their mortality and getting a last chance to do something exciting before departing this Earth. There are even organizations dedicated to such pursuits, such as Make-A-Wish whose mission is to "Create life-changing wishes for children with critical illnesses." As wonderful as granting wishes sounds, it gives the impression that fulfilling wishes is a near-death activity. Thus, the bucket list, which concentrates on wish fulfillment, has a negative connotation. This often leads people to think they don't need to have such a list—at least not yet. Whatever impression you have of a bucket list, I can assure you that it is a positive, enjoyable tool to use when planning out fun experiences for your life. A life lived to the fullest includes many bucket list items that should be enjoyed.

Enjoyment of Life

"So, I recommend having fun, because there is nothing better for people in this world than to eat, drink, and enjoy life. That way they will experience some happiness along with all the hard work God gives them under the sun." (Ecclesiastes 8:15 NLT) Wow, "having fun", "enjoying life", "happiness." This scripture acknowledges that we should and do work hard in this life but are also allowed to experience fun and enjoyment. Some people feel guilty about enjoying life, others feel the need to people-please. This selflessness is admirable yet unnecessary. When we enjoy our lives, we become more enjoyable to be around. We can even make fulfilling our bucket list a group event. It does not have to be a selfish endeavor.

Do I have a bucket list? You betcha! Have I been working on it? Of Course! Each year I make sure to cross something off that list. If it is a true bucket list then it will take a while to complete. Often, it means saving money, such as saving up for that African Safari trip. Many times, it involves an element of fear such as going skydiving. Maybe it involves some risk taking such as starting your own business. Perhaps it is fitness-related, as in weightlifting (no way you can rush this) or getting married (which can depend on someone else). The time to start living that list is now.

What is a Bucket List?

Perhaps you already have a bucket list or know someone who does. Many people have a mental bucket list kept in their heads but make no conscious effort to work on it. It may sound counterintuitive to have to work on your fun items but if you don't, then they are not likely to just occur on their own. When you decide to go on a vacation does it just happen? Of course not! You have decisions to make about destinations, air travel to book, car rentals to reserve, etc. It doesn't just happen; you need to plan it. Sure, there will be opportunities in life that present themselves, but these will be few and far between. Why wait for opportunities when you can create them?

So, what is a bucket list? To answer this question, we need to first look at the term. Apparently, the term "bucket list" was coined by screenwriter Justin Zackham in 1999 when he was working on the film *The Bucket List* which was released in 2007. In the film, two terminally ill patients, portrayed by Jack Nicholson and Morgan Freeman, were trying to fulfill wishes they had for their lives before passing away or "kicking the bucket" to use a slang term. In searching this term, it seems that people are familiar with the concept of making lists of the things they would like to do in life. In the television show *Yes Dear*, Jimmy has a near-death experience and thus the discussion of his list ensues. But as I reviewed this episode, I heard him refer to it as "A list before dying".

> **Think About It:**
> **If you could have one wish granted before you died, what would that wish be?**

A bucket list focuses on life. It is a list of items that you want to accomplish during your lifetime. It is a personal list. Your bucket list, ironically, is a live document, meaning you may alter this list at any time. After all, it is about your wishes. Do you have a bucket list? A list of things you want to do or see before you die? You know "I've always wanted to _____". Perhaps you have childhood fantasies such as "I want to be a fireman!" Maybe you were inspired by someone in college: "I'd like to join the Peace Corps" or "Write a great American novel". Maybe you have goals such as owning a home or a fancy car. Whether you write it out in list form making it an official bucket list or just have big dreams in your mind, you need a list.

Bucket List versus the To-Do List

When we talk about bucket list items, thoughts of adventure and excitement appear. When we talk about our to-do list, thoughts of grocery shopping and carpooling should come to mind. There will always be those gray areas that blend the two. For instance, I have a list of items I want to accomplish at my house. Getting that rock garden completed is a project. I doubt, however, that I would put it on my weekly to-do list as it will take some time to finish. I also don't think that when this rock garden is built, it will be a memory significant enough to be remembered when my life flashes before my eyes. Bucket list items should be those that come to mind when reviewing your life on your deathbed. They are the experiences you think of as you tell others that you lived your life and that it was, indeed, a full life.

Having a beautiful house may be important to you. There may be a part of this home, such as a landscaped backyard, which provides the setting for hosting family events which bring joy to others. Do not be rigid in fitting all your life activities into boxes. If something blends into another area of your life that is fine. The important aspect is to lead a life of meaning, with a purpose, honoring God while enjoying yourself along the way.

Do You Really Need a Bucket List?

We live our lives in a somewhat mundane manner. Go to work, workout, cook dinner, watch TV, socialize a little on the weekends, go to church, then repeat. If we are not careful, we may wake up one day and realize that life has passed us by, and that our dream, which lay dormant in our heart, went unfulfilled. We need to turn these dreams, or long-term goals (which we will cover later in our goal-setting chapter) into reality. It is with our bucket list that we sprinkle in life's exciting events. Hmm, I think I can hear your arguments now: "I don't have time to work on bucket list items." "I don't have the money for it, I am barely getting by as it is." "It sure must be nice." It can feel frustrating to see others have adventures when we are just trying to pay our bills.

Sprinkles

Our bucket list is all about sprinkles. If we never go zip lining but are financially independent with a loving family, I would say that is an awesome life. If we were to only engage in bucket list adventures but not reach any of our spiritual or career aspirations, we would definitely have life backward. The bucket list items are the icing, sprinkles, and cherry on top of our cake. Sometimes when life starts to feel dull, and it will, you need to throw a bucket list item in there to bring back the excitement in life. But do you really need this? I guess not. We don't need sprinkles, but they sure are nice to have.

If you find yourself feeling too busy for sprinkles, then it is time to engage in some self-reflection. Why do you not have time? It worries me when people state that they don't have time for themselves. These are also the people who report feeling unhappy and dissatisfied with their lives. Usually, these people report feeling trapped in life circumstances. Honestly, there will be times when you are confined in life situations: taking care of a terminally ill loved one, raising children, adhering to financial obligations, etc. There will be certain commitments in life that may take some time to resolve. Life contains a series of problems and resolutions. Sometimes these hardships are for a season and sometimes they are long term. Although it may be difficult to carve out the time, make sure you never deny yourself prayer and worship with God. You need this time with the Lord. It truly is an investment in yourself because He will give you strength and lead you in the right direction, as long as you allow Him to guide you. You must allow this time to invest in yourself because no one else can do it for you. It is your job to take care of you.

Benefits of a Bucket List

There are many benefits to having a bucket list. It gives you something to look forward to. A bucket list is an excellent conversation piece, whether it is discussing your upcoming adventure or telling a story about a recent experience. It increases self-esteem, you just did something cool, and made that experience happen. Fulfilling list items means breaking the mundane, day-in-day-out cycle, it can be inspiring to others and shows people that you are a go-getter. Most importantly, it allows you to live life to the fullest!

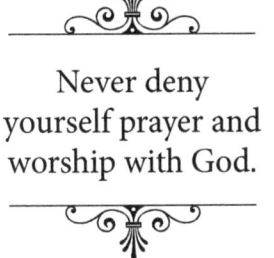

> Never deny yourself prayer and worship with God.

The Bucket List and Self-Care

Bubble baths. Facials. Mani-pedis. Ahh, self-care. NOT! These items, although decadent and enjoyable, are merely marketing strategies. Spend money on these items and it means that you are taking care of yourself–NOPE! Don't get me wrong. There are times when I really do need a pedicure, but self-care is more simplistic. Self-care is not about decadence; it is about survival. Self-care means getting that extra hour of sleep when you are tired. It means using paper plates occasionally, so you don't have to spend time cleaning up after dinner. It means doing curbside rather than grocery shopping when you are overextended in terms of time. This type of self-care, however, is only a temporary fix. You can't sleep in every weekend and frequently picking up fast food can quickly lead to a decline in health, but there are times when you just need a break. This is where consistent self-reflection about our priorities is required. It means setting boundaries and telling people "No" when you are feeling overwhelmed. We may want to be a team player and help others but if agreeing to help means we give a halfhearted effort with a bad attitude, then maybe it is best to decline. In the same respect, self-care does not mean selfishness. You do not have to be at 100% before you can help others. We don't want to get to the point where we wait for everything to be perfect before we attempt to engage in meaningful activities.

> Self-care is not about decadence; it is about survival.

Part of self-care means making your own heart happy. Choosing to do something on your bucket list is self-care. The cool thing is you can do something on your bucket list involving your family and/or friends. Perhaps you have always wanted to go to Spain. I am pretty sure that when you envisioned doing this you did not picture yourself going solo. You can fulfill this bucket list item by taking your family to Spain. What a wonderful way to bond with the family by planning such a trip. You can fulfill a bucket list item, refilling your empty cup while making an investment in your family relationships. The memories created will last a lifetime.

Prayer

"May he grant your heart's desires and make all your plans succeed." (Psalm 20:4 NLT) This psalm from King David shows me that it is okay to pray to God for my wants. It shows me that I need to pray to God for His help in making my plans a reality. Some people feel guilty when they pray for their own needs let alone for their wants. I have even heard some people state that it is selfish to pray for yourself. When I pray, I do pray for myself. Don't get me wrong, I pray for others daily, but I also pray for myself. If I'm not in a good place, how can I be there for others? It is also freeing, to know that it is okay to advocate for myself through prayer.

What Are You Waiting For?

Are you delaying working on your dreams and wishes for your life? If you are putting your life on pause, then I must ask–"What are you waiting for?" You cannot wait until retirement to start working toward your dreams. Why would you want to wait? We do not know how much time we have left, only the Lord knows. We do not know how much vitality or how many healthy years we have to complete certain tasks in life. We have all heard stories of elderly people completing some pretty awesome adventures. I remember when at 90 years old, former President Bush Sr. went skydiving to celebrate his birthday. The reason we see these stories in the news is that they are out of the norm. As we age, our physical abilities diminish. This is not to give you permission to decline certain dreams because you are of a certain age.

I refuse to let my age define me. However, in reality, would you be physically able to skydive when you are ninety? If the answer is yes, then let me ask you another question—"Do you see yourself *enjoying* skydiving at age ninety?" Our goals involve not only living out our dreams but being able to enjoy those dreams. Don't wait until retirement age to start living. By the way, the ninetieth birthday jump was not President Bush's first skydive.

In Reverend John Roberts' book, *Caught Red Handed*, he talks about keeping track of the number of days we have left and making the most of them. Our time here on earth is limited, so we don't want to waste any of it. Does that mean that if we come to the end of our lives with an incomplete bucket list our life is a waste? Of course not! This book is about living your life to the fullest, living with no regrets, maximizing your time, and getting the most out of life. For me, this starts with a bucket list.

Listen to Your Heart, Listen to God

When we make lists of our wants, many people have short lists, not because they lack these desires but because they are not accustomed to looking and listening within themselves. "Now then, stand still and see this great thing the LORD is about to do before your eyes!" (1 Samuel 12:16 NIV) I love the wonderful feeling of anticipation that this scripture evokes. It brings a sense of hope. If the Lord is about to do something "great", it certainly is beyond my imagination. This scripture also tells us to "stand still and see", this speaks to me. In the hustle and bustle of daily life, it is easy to miss God's voice. Taking time out to talk to God may feel like a sacrifice of your time, being still and listening for His response is difficult. We are always on the go, running from one place to another, with demands on us at work and home. In the rare downtime, most of us fill that small void with music, television, and scrolling social media. If we choose to embrace solace, we can be easily distracted by chirps from our phones. Standing still is not something we are accustomed to.

Listening is a lost art. In conversations, we are accustomed to planning out what we are going to say next rather than focusing on what we are responding to. It is important to allow yourself quiet time to reflect upon the direction you want your life to take. Look deep into your heart and be honest about your answer. Ask God to give you guidance. This last part is the most difficult yet crucial, take the time to listen to His response.

There Are Many Kinds of Buckets

One size fits all. Not when it comes to bucket lists. A bucket list is individualized, and unlike clothing, it is not one size fits all. Just as you can outgrow that outfit, you can also outgrow your bucket list items. There are many types of bucket lists. A general individual bucket list, a couple's bucket list, a family bucket list, even a friendship bucket list. You can get silly and create a "ride" bucket list. Examples can include riding a: horse, camel, elephant, dog sled, motorcycle, jet ski, helicopter, you get the idea. You can also create one for:

- career
- travel
- Christmas
- Summer
- school (high school, college, grad school)
- exotic foods to eat
- adventure
- sports related
- concert experiences
- books to read

This list goes on and on. Tailor it to your own interests. Just as collectors can acquire many various items (coins, baseball cards, etc.) the bucket list is an attempt at collecting experiences.

Sharing Your Buckets

Whether you have an actual bucket list or just several ideas in your head about cool things you want to do, you know that these are not everyday types of activities. Some of these ideas may seem crazy, some may be things you know others may also want to try. Have you shared your bucket list with your loved ones? You may be surprised to discover the fantasies your friends and family have. These lists may inspire you to add to your own list. They may also cause you to combine forces and experience your items together. Or better yet, you may be that influence helping a friend or family member to fulfill their bucket list items. Just the act of discussing your list items with friends and family can create a bond with your loved ones. This is a time for non-judgmental sharing. Asking someone how they think they will ever afford such a trip or be fit enough to complete that 10k is not the point. You are listening to the desires of their heart. You want to provide encouragement, not squash anyone's hopes. If a person truly wants something, they will find a way to make it happen. Maybe it will not look the way it was originally pictured, but they can make it happen. Remember, your bucket list is a tool, use it to get closer to loved ones. Before you even begin checking off those list items, your bucket list can bring happiness.

Travel

We can't discuss bucket lists without mentioning travel. Most people will have bucket list items involving travel. Traveling is a way to maximize your bucket list experiences. It gives you the ability to stack your buckets. You can check off a mode of transportation, such as taking a cruise to a place you want to visit, and then fulfill another bucket list item while you are there through an excursion.

When you travel you get to:

1. See new places (cool things).
2. Have unique transportation such as: doing a road trip, traveling by RV, train (a beautiful way to see the country by the way), ship, or plane.
3. Getting away from daily responsibilities.
4. Having an excuse for decadence.

5. Enjoy the accommodations: booking a vacation rental or hotel with a pool, staying with friends or family (great quality time!), or obtaining lodging in a cabin or even a youth hostel.
6. Doing things you would not normally do: being your vacation self, such as talking to strangers, trying new activities, wearing outfits you would not usually wear, being with your loved ones all day, and breaking your diet.

Creating Your Own Bucket List

The most powerful part of creating your bucket list is putting it down on paper. Whether you go old school with paper and pen (my preferred method) or enter it in the computer, it must be a documented list. Sorry, no more keeping those ideas in your head. If this is a true bucket list it must be written out. Otherwise, it is just a bunch of ideas floating in your noggin. Fleeting thoughts are not life-changing, bucket list items are. When thinking about your list, several items will most likely jump to mind. Putting your items into categories can help clarify your ideas. The reason many people do not follow through with their actions is due to lack of clarity. Saying that you want to do something fun and exciting is subjective. Phrasing it in this manner implies you are waiting for someone else to give you the idea. Why use someone else's brain when you can use your own? Sure, you can go to other people for inspiration, but no one truly understands your heart's desires except you and the Lord. I find that most bucket list items fall into seven categories:

Experiences, Ownership, Kindness, Creations, Learning, Travel, and Accomplishments. After reviewing many bucket lists, I have found that I must give an honorable mention to the eight possible category—Quirky. Not everyone will have this eighth category which is the reason it has an honorable mention.

Experiences – Getting out there and doing something. Examples include white water rafting, bungee jumping, and driving a race car.

Ownership – These are the items that you would like to own someday. They can range from an expensive wardrobe to a house, motorcycle, or boat.

Kindness – This area involves helping others. Remember earlier when I talked about not needing to feel selfish.

Living Your Best Life While Embracing Christianity

Inspiration

Just to help you get that brain working in a creative way, I compiled a list of 100 possible Bucket List Ideas for you to think about. Hopefully, you will find interest in a few of these ideas and will then tweak them to make them your own.

100 Bucket List Ideas

- Skydive
- Scuba dive
- Mountain climb
- White water rafting
- Ziplining
- Zorbing
- Be a beauty pageant contestant
- Bungee jump
- Go on a mission trip
- Parasailing
- Visit all 50 states
- Learn archery
- Grand Canyon donkey ride
- Hot air balloon ride
- Fly a plane
- Visit all 7 continents
- Drive a racecar
- Swim with dolphins
- Go dog sledding
- Be an extra in a movie
- Go to clown school
- Publish a book
- Baseball game at Wrigley Field
- See the Running of the Bulls
- Attend a Comic-Con
- Learn to play chess
- Take Christmas White House tour
- Set a Guinness Book record
- Go to an escape room
- See the Northern Lights
- Go to the Olympics
- Learn origami
- Climb the Statue of Liberty
- Win salesperson of the year
- Join the Peace Corps
- Milk a cow

- Go ax throwing
- Hit a hole in one
- Take a selfie with a celebrity
- Win a Christmas decor contest
- Attend a live dog show
- Read the Bible in its entirety
- Hula dance in Hawaii
- Learn to play piano
- Be a game show contestant
- Take a trapeze lesson
- Go to a Dude Ranch
- Master a yo-yo trick
- Get a patent on an invention
- Be a room mother for a year
- Learn Karate
- Buy a house
- Get married
- Have children
- Become a business owner
- Run a marathon
- Take a cross-country roundtrip
- Take a cruise
- Attend the Superbowl
- Go camping
- Go to Mardi Gras
- Get a tattoo
- Spend the night in a treehouse
- Go skiing
- Be at ideal weight
- Donate blood
- Sing karaoke
- Ride a horse
- Speak at a conference
- Earn a college degree
- Shoot a gun
- Make an online video
- Be part of a live TV audience
- Host & cook Thanksgiving dinner
- See Mount Rushmore
- Adopt a shelter dog
- Host a foreign exchange student
- See the Leaning Tower of Pisa
- Take a dream family vacation
- See Taylor Swift in concert
- Learn sign language

The Bucket List: Adding Sprinkles to Your Life

- **Donate hair to charity**
- **Go on a Police ride along**
- **Donate wedding dress to charity**
- **Own a sports car**
- **Learn to surf**
- **Ride a motorcycle**
- **Learn to juggle**
- **Take a professional family portrait**
- **Eat meal cooked by a Michelin-star chef**
- **Bowl a turkey**
- **Sit in the box at a sports event**
- **Go deep-sea fishing**
- **Snorkel**
- **Sensory deprivation tank session**
- **Bet on a horse race**
- **Go ice skating**
- **Chase a tornado**
- **Walk on a suspension bridge**
- **Sit in an emergency exit aisle of a plane**

My Bucket List Worksheet

Experiences

_____
_____
_____
_____

Ownership

_____
_____
_____
_____

Kindness

_____
_____
_____
_____

Creations

_____
_____
_____
_____

Learning

_____
_____
_____
_____

Accomplishments

_____
_____
_____
_____

Quirky

_____
_____
_____
_____

Checking Items Off the List

You've created your bucket list! Congratulations! Just having your personalized bucket list written out should give you a good feeling because you have some exciting things to look forward to. Now, you get the opportunity to execute that list. The best way to do this is to:

1. Prioritize your list of items, and acknowledge the items which are absolutes, those that if you never completed would cause you to feel regret.
2. Choose the one(s) you would like to accomplish first (within the next year).

Make a plan for this item, taking into account the resources of research, time, people, and money.

Resources

If you have created your list, and are now reading it over and feel overwhelmed, don't despair. You are not alone. This list is designed to be challenging. Remember if the items were everyday occurrences, they would be on your to-do list not your bucket list. Although some items can be accomplished in a weekend, such as singing karaoke, most should be special occasion events which will require strategic planning. Bucket list items will require resources. Research, Time, People, and Money are the main resources you will need.

Research – You may have items on your list that you find intriguing but have no idea how to carry them out. Riding a camel sounds awesome but where do I find a camel? Fortunately, we have the internet at our disposal. It may take a while to find out how we can have access to that camel. Are you seeking a camel in the U.S., or do you want to go all out and make this an exotic trip to Egypt to do so? Whatever your desire is, just make sure you do the proper research so that carrying out your bucket list item is everything you want it to be.

Time – Do you have the time available to carry out your bucket list items? Oftentimes, people experience time conflicts with work commitments. If you are an accountant, then attending a festival in early April is going to require a great deal of finagling. If you are a teacher, planning a vacation in September will just not work out. Do you have vacation time saved up so that you can go on your adventures?

People – It may sound odd that I have listed people under the resource section but hear me out. It is important to note that people are our most important resource. You may have a coworker or fellow church member who has done the very list item you are seeking to accomplish. There may be a friend who knows of the cheapest time to fly out of your city. We also may need assistance in terms of coworkers taking over some responsibilities for us, or relatives watching the kids. There may even be a neighbor who can hook you up with an inexpensive dog sitter to take care of your pooch while you go on your excursion. The idea of people under resources can also include finding your partners in crime. Although traveling alone can be empowering, it is also fun to take a trip with friends, bonding while doing wild and memorable things. So, in terms of resources, have you figured out who you would like to be your accomplice in your next list item?

Money – Everything in life, it seems, boils down to money. Your bucket list item may be expensive and thus you will need to budget for it. Remember that when you do research, you may be able to find group discounts, coupons, or perhaps a bartering arrangement to help ease the expenses. Think about the requirements for your list items. When you go to Pisa to see the Leaning Tower, do you want to stay in a four-star hotel or are you willing to stay in a youth hostel? Obviously, there is a major difference in cost between the two. Your choice depends on the vision you have for your experience. Depending on the cost, you may even consider getting a side gig expressly to earn money for this experience. Sometimes your side gig can be an experience all in itself. (Such as when I supplemented my income one Spring by working for the Easter Bunny!)

Can the Bucket Rust?

Do bucket lists change over time? Of course, they do! If you view the bucket list of one of your children, you may see items such as graduating high school and owning a car. Items that as an adult seem very attainable, but as a teen these are a big deal. As an adult, you may have items in which you have lost interest and that is okay. Change your list. There should be something on the list that sparks your interest. Major life events may influence what you want on your bucket list and may cause you to alter some items.

Going back to the episode of *Yes Dear*: on his list, Jimmy had stated that he wanted to sleep with a supermodel. He wrote his list when he was single. Now that he was married, he altered his list item. He changed it from sleeping with a supermodel to dancing with a supermodel. It is your list, and you can alter it as you see fit. It is up to you if you choose to share the content with others. You do not have to explain your list choices to anyone, nor apologize or feel bad for altering any of your items. A bucket list is meant to add spice to your life and increase your self-esteem.

Please don't feel pressured to put things on your list just because it sounds like the thing to do. The items on your list should make you feel giddy. Once you check them off it should provide a sense of accomplishment and pride that stays with you for years. If you are merely putting things on your list because it is what everyone else is doing, then you will not benefit, and it misses the entire point of having a bucket list. This list is about you and your interests.

My Bucket List Worksheet

Your Turn:

Without limiting yourself to time constraints, money, or the opinions of others, list five items you would like to check off your bucket list in the next three years.

1. _____

   _____

2. _____

   _____

3. _____

   _____

4. _____

   _____

5. _____

   _____

"Die with memories, not dreams."

- Unknown

Chapter 5

Vision Boards: Manifesting Your Dreams

Vision boards and manifesting your dreams seem to be all the buzz these days. Exploring one's hopes and dreams, along with the possibility's life brings, is an exciting process. Looking at my vision board gives me a glimpse into my future. I enjoy gazing at those possibilities. Making a vision board is a creative process. It is fun and simple, but most people never create one. They are definitely missing out.

Are You a Simpleton?

Have you fallen into simpleton syndrome? What is simpleton syndrome you ask? It is when you have tasks that are crucial to your success that are simple to complete, yet you choose, either on purpose or by default, not to complete those tasks. The problem with simple is that most people often do not follow through. Drinking water is simple, right? Then why don't we do this? Saving ten percent of your income is simple, but do you do it? Walking thirty minutes each day, this can be accomplished by even the most out-of-shape people, a very simple task, so why is this not being done? Sometimes when something is simple, we take for granted that we can always do it. You may belong to a 24-hour gym but never seem to find the time to go there, yet often it is the gym with limited hours, that forces you to put it into your schedule and make it work. This goes back to priorities. Make your schedule and place these simple tasks on it.

Some people don't pursue their dreams because they are afraid of being too "put together". I know that may sound weird, but people really can experience a fear of success. Everyone enjoys that pleasant feeling of daydreaming about their fantasy life. Taking yourself a step out of that daydream, to make this wish a reality, can be scary. If it does not work out, what happens to your happy little fantasy? What if the dream does work out? Now there are expectations that must be met. In his article, *Fear of Success & 3 Steps to Overcome It,* Eli Straw reports that fear of failure, perfectionism, and self-sabotage all play roles in a person's fear of success. Being aware that you may be sabotaging your success is crucial to turning your actions around. Acknowledge that you are worthy of success and that with success there will be failures along the way. It is through these failures that we grow.

Goals

Many people say they have goals but very few have them written down. It is so simple to write them down that people don't do it. After all, why would you need to document your desires? You don't need to be reminded of them because it is what you want, right? Wrong! How many times have you heard someone talk about a dream they had that went unfulfilled because life got in the way? Yes, life happens. Things we could never imagine, be it good and bad, will occur that throw off our well-intentioned plans. Have those goals in front of you so you do not lose focus when life throws out a curveball. Once you reach a certain age, you grow to realize that nothing should be taken for granted. If you do not focus on your dreams now, then when? There will always be things in life that will throw you off course. Think about having the desire to lose weight. Whether it is to avoid negative health issues or obtain the attractiveness of being slender, it is a popular notion many people can relate to. Now let's say you have a series of celebrations. Of course, celebrations often involve food and understandably you want to indulge. No judgment here! But next thing you know, the month is over, and you have not lost any weight. Hopefully, you have not gone in the other direction and gained any weight. We can easily rationalize that enjoying life is about active participation in such events. However, if you have your goals in front of you, where you can view them daily, you can plan for events while working toward your objective. In having a strategy for attaining your goals, you will have a means of dealing with obstacles and when you do go off course you can get right back on your road to success. Having a contingency plan, also known as a backup plan, can give you peace of mind in case things do not work out according to your design. The road to success is rarely a straight shot, it is often winding with unforeseen obstacles. If it were an easy, and straight path, then everyone would be a success. Start aligning yourself with others who share your aspirations. You can discuss strategies and encourage one another.

> Have those goals in front of you so you do not lose focus when life throws out a curveball.

What is a Vision Board?

So, what is a vision board anyway? A vision board is a way of documenting the dreams you have for your life. These may be long-term dreams such as getting married and starting a family, or short-term dreams such as taking dance lessons or going on a vacation. A vision board is a *visual* representation of your dreams which you will be turning into reality. To me, a vision board is the opposite of a memory book. A memory book contains photos of past experiences. If these photos have made it into an actual photo book and not just on your phone, then they are probably significant to you in some way. The memory book deals with past dreams. Perhaps you even participated in the scrapbook craze from many years ago. In scrapbooking, you choose a memorable experience to commemorate and select the most relevant photos to represent the experience. Of course, in scrapbooking, you make the pictures cute by framing them and adding embellishments. The aspect I enjoyed most about scrapbooking, however, was the written comments that accompanied those pictures, discussing the significance of each particular photo.

A vision board, on the other hand, deals with current and future dreams. A vision board is a tool used to turn dreams into goals. In other words, to make your dreams your reality. By now we know that goals need to be written out. A vision board goes one step further than this. With a vision board, you are attaching pictures to represent these goals. In the process of handwriting, you are engaging both a kinesthetic and visual element of the brain which will work in conjunction with the pictures you have chosen. Our mind has a tendency to focus on images before the written word. I think this is the reason for the appeal of social media where we can gaze upon pictures posted by our friends. When we dream of our goals we create a picture of them in our minds. If you want to live in a beautiful house, what does that look like to you? Give me ten people with this dream, and I will show you ten different visual representations.

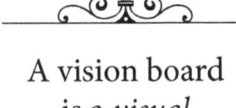

> A vision board is a *visual* representation of your dreams which you will be turning into reality.

Ownership

The concept of personal responsibility, taking ownership of your life and how it unfolds, is an integral part of attaining your dreams. There are certain things in life that we just can't delegate to others. Oh, how I wish I could get someone to do my dieting for me or sit in that dentist's chair to get that tooth filled. There are experiences in life that you must personally endure. Many times, it is through these "I'll have to do it on my own" endeavors that promote the most growth within us. These do not have to be negative experiences. For instance, only you can create this vision board. It is the process of its creation that is mind-altering. You are matching pictures to the goals you have already written on paper. Perhaps you may be the type of person who enjoys doing creative things and may really get into this vision board as a creative project. Yes, for you, it can be a trip to the craft store or pulling out those old scrapbook materials. If this is the case, then go for it. Enjoy the process. Maybe you want to invite friends over and make an evening of it. The more invested you are in this process the better. It makes me think of those painting places that are popular today. Friends get together at a painting venue (BYOB) to paint the picture of the day with their own brush strokes. Most of the fun is in the process. At the end of the session, you get to take your painting home. At this point, some people may just trash it because the fun was in the creating process. Others, however, may choose to display it. In displaying it, they now have a unique piece of artwork that shows their personality and is a reminder of a good time with friends. Although it is the same picture for each person, you discover how unique your finished painting looks in comparison to that of your peers.

Embrace your uniqueness. You may have many similarities with your friends, but God created us individually with our own special qualities which are unique unto ourselves. There is no one in this world exactly like you. The same goes for your goals. If you and your best friend both have intentions of losing twenty pounds those results will look different on each of you. You have a different vision of a dream job than your cohorts. Even the idea of a Hawaiian get-a-way will look different for each person. Your idea of that perfect vacation will not necessarily be similar to your spouse's idea of that same destination. So, try to enjoy this process of making your individualized vision board.

> **Think About It:**
> Do you have a dream that seems almost impossible?

Why Do I Need a Vision Board?

If you have a dream in your heart that seems almost impossible, then you need a vision board. You need to be able to visualize yourself accomplishing your dream. "Look", you may be thinking, "I'm not a crafty person, I like to keep things simple." I get it. I must admit that I have unfinished scrapbooks in my closet. The actual act of creating this board may not be appealing to you. You may not want to have an actual board that others may see. That's fine, instead of a board, you can create a vision book. Either way, you need both a written and pictorial representation of your dreams and goals.

We do not just create our vision boards, we use them. Using a vision board is part of a multisensory approach. We use our sense of *vision* when we look at our board (or book) every day. We *see* the pictures and words we have written. We use our *auditory* senses when we *verbalize* our dreams and goals out loud and *hear* our own voices making these proclamations. We have the *kinesthetic* experience of physically *making* our vision board as well as remembering the process of doing this. We involve God when we *pray* over these goals. All these actions help us to visualize ourselves attaining our dreams. In Proverbs 23:7 it states "…for as he thinks in his heart, so is he…" (TLB) We need to keep our focus on our goals.

"Where there is no prophetic vision the people cast off restraint, but blessed is he who keeps the law." (Proverbs 29:18 ESV) This scripture shows me that we all need guidance. We need to focus on those dreams that God has put in our hearts. God does not want us to lead a life of self-indulgence and greed. Carrying out our goals allows us a means to which we can bless others. Perhaps you have a goal of earning a certain salary. Why do you want this increased income? There may be a lifestyle you want to lead that requires a certain figure of income. Part of this new lifestyle should also include gratitude to God. The more money you earn the more you will be able to tithe and bless others.

Now Is the Time

We are putting short-term goals on our vision boards. A short-term goal would focus on dreams we can accomplish within the next year to year-and-a-half. There will be items that are long-term, and these can be placed on your board as well. The focus dreams should be those for which you can accomplish in the next year. These should not be easy; they should involve tasks that will stretch you by getting you out of your comfort zone. You will need to work on these goals diligently to complete them. You should have goals that need praying over and that require God's help. If your tasks are too easy, then it will not be that big a deal when it is accomplished. You want to experience growth through this process. Completion of your goals should give you a sense of pride. Notice I said pride, not arrogance. We want to be proud of our accomplishments while retaining our humility. For all things that we accomplish are due to blessings from the Lord. Having these short-term objectives will help us to act with a sense of urgency that can be applied to working on our long-term tasks. As you complete your vision board activities this year, you will find it easier to conquer your long-term desires. Long-term goals (those taking five or more years to complete) can be broken down into small steps. So, when you see your long-term goal on your vision board ask yourself how you can work on it this week. We should be doing something every day to get closer to that vision. With each move you make, ask yourself if this is getting you closer to your dream or further away from it.

How to Create Your Vision Board

Here are some supplies you will need to create your vision board: a corkboard, poster board, or artist book (however you choose to display your vision), scissors, adhesive, and push pins. If you are crafty and enjoy this process, you can use scrapbooking paper or construction paper as a background for your board. You will also need pens or markers (whatever you want to use to write out your dreams and goals) and paper to write out your vision. You may even want to purchase or make numbers to prioritize the dreams in your life.

I have saved the most important for last–pictures! You will need pictorial representations of your dreams. You can cut pictures out of magazines, brochures, or screenshots from social media. My favorite way to do this is to search for my dream online, screenshot it, and then print it out as if it were a real picture.

It can be enjoyable to search for pictures of your dreams. Just make sure you do not get stuck in this phase of the process. For instance, if your goal is to get married, you may want to put a wedding dress as one of the pictures on your board. Make sure you do not get too caught up in finding the perfect dress, unless of course, your dream is for something very specific. Set a time limit, say no longer than an hour, to search online. We all know how time flies on the web, you experience clickbait and the next thing you know the evening can be gone. You do not want to be distracted from your purpose. The enemy is working hard to keep us distracted. Remember that you need a visual to represent your dream and then you are also going to write out your goal. At any time, if you find a picture that better represents that dream, then switch out the pictures. Think of your social media accounts, you change your profile pictures every so often, right? It may depend on your mood or seasonal events. It's okay to switch out your pictures on your vision board as well, especially as you get closer to your goal, and become more specific about that goal. Just get some pictures on that board! You may also want to frame your pictures. If using a poster board or an artist's book, then you won't need to do this. As an added bonus, you may include an inspirational statement or scripture that speaks out to you, providing increased motivation.

Living Your Best Life While Embracing Christianity

    Try to refrain from using the cutesy stickers/embellishments that are often used in scrapbooking. The focus needs to be on the pictures and written goals, not the decor. You may also find it useful to put a picture of Jesus or simply the cross on your board. This will remind you that it is God who is in control. God gives you the energy and resources to complete your goals. You can also choose to put a picture of yourself on your board. It helps to make your dream seem accessible. If your dream is a family vacation to Hawaii, you can take a picture of yourself wearing a lei or perhaps a grass skirt. You can superimpose your picture over a Hawaiian landscape. Next, it is time for preparation. Just as a chef may do their meal prep by chopping vegetables before starting to cook, so must you do your vision prep before putting things on the board.

No Judgement Zone

List your dreams and goals that you hope to accomplish within the next year to year and a half. This vision board is for the upcoming year and there needs to be a sense of urgency in terms of working towards your goals. Of course, you will have long-term dreams and you can break those down in chunk-sized increments when working on your goals, but our vision board will focus on the present. There is a quote I have found interesting from Bill Gates: "We always overestimate the change that will occur in the next two years and underestimate the change that will occur in the next 10. Don't let yourself be lulled into inaction."

Try to come up with about five goals for the upcoming year. I usually would tell you to go for everything, have unlimited dreams, and not restrict yourself but there is a reason I want you to limit it to five. If you have too many goals to focus on, then your attention will be divided. Since you want to attain your goals in the upcoming year, you want to have the time and focus to really put effort into working on them. Focus on goals which can be reasonably accomplished in this twelve-to-eighteen-month timeframe. Think about what is most important to you. What goal, if accomplished, will have a positive impact on other areas of your life? For example, maybe you have goals of getting that promotion at work, learning to ice skate, and traveling to Alaska. Each person's lifestyle is different, but in my opinion, the goal of getting that promotion at work will have an impact on the other areas of this person's life. Usually, a promotion will lead to a raise. In obtaining that raise it will also help the person pay for those ice-skating lessons and provide funds for that trip to Alaska. Or maybe, one of your goals is the one we discussed earlier, to lose weight. Losing weight can benefit you in terms of your health, increase your confidence at work as well as in social settings, and make it easier for you to get around and explore when you do go on your travels. I am not saying that the smaller goals should not be worked on, but I am saying to get the most out of the goals you choose to work towards.

Now that you have your top five goals and the pictures to represent them. I want you to write out your dream using positive present-tense language. For example, if you would like to publish a book you would write "I am a published author". You may have a picture of a book to go with this or you can have your picture taken holding a book which would represent a book you wrote. You can take a picture of the house you want. Write out "I own this house". In this process, you are attaching ownership to your goal. You are envisioning yourself attaining it. Attach both the picture and written goal together on the board. Just a reminder here, a goal is a dream with a deadline. Your deadline, or target date, is twelve to eighteen months from now but please don't put the same date for each goal. This may mean that you want to accomplish one of the goals by your birthday or by the end of the school year or on an anniversary date. As you attach those pictures with written goal statements, add the accomplishment date by the picture as well.

A Sight to Be Seen!

Who needs to see this vision board? Just you. The actual vision board itself is important and you need to have it in a place where you look at it daily. You are certainly welcome to share it with others and most probably, your family will eventually see it, but you are not obligated to share these dreams with others. There will always be naysayers who may discourage you. This vision board is a tool to encourage you to focus on attaining your dreams, not a vehicle to open yourself up to confidence-crushing. This is a vision board representing your personal dreams.

One important aspect of the vision board is that it gives us a multisensory approach to acknowledge the goals we need to be working on. We need to see the picture of what we are working on, read the goal, say the goal out loud and pray over it. It needs to be seared in our brains. The more it is to the front of our brain the more likely we will be working on it. Success does not happen haphazardly. For example, a college student does not just obtain a degree, they must strategize the courses to be taken and then do the work required. The same is true for your dreams.

Place your vision board in a place where you will see it every day, preferably several times a day. Take a picture of it so that you will have it on your phone for times when you are not home, as many of us these days are constantly on the go. For those of you who wish to keep it private due to unsupportive family or household members, make the vision book. Take a picture of each page. As long as you are viewing it at least daily it will inspire you and keep the vision alive.

Manifestation

Another buzz word—manifestation. What does this mean? It means that what we think about, we bring into our lives. Does this sound familiar... You decide you want a certain kind of car in a specific color, and next thing you know, all you seem to see on the road is that particular vehicle. Did you make that happen? Not really, you just made yourself conscious of the car and now are able to see it in reality whereas you were not previously paying attention. The same process is occurring here. This is called the frequency of illusion also known as the Baader-Meinhof Phenomenon. You are bringing your dreams to the front of your mind. You are hyper-focused on obtaining this goal therefore you are looking for opportunities to take advantage of to fulfill this desire. We make so many choices in our daily lives that we tend to go on autopilot. By focusing intently on our goals, we start to recognize these opportunities and thus use them to our advantage.

Prioritize the dreams you wish to bring to fruition during the next twelve to eighteen months. Write these dreams out in goal form, find a visual representation that matches it, and then put it all together on a board. Although the process of creating this vision board is important, this is only half the process. This is not a one-and-done deal. You must have this board in a place where you will view it every morning when you awaken and every evening before you go to sleep. You must read your goals aloud and pray over them.

In her book, *Visual Prayer: How to Create a Spiritual Vision Board*, Dr. Crystal Green Brown reports that "The spiritual vision board process can be viewed as an ongoing record of your prayer requests, communication and connection with God." Praying over these goals and asking the Lord that these goals be within His will is a way to grow closer to Him. When you pray about this, take the time to listen to His response. Many times when we pray, we make it a monologue, say what we want to say, end the prayer, and off we go to our next activity. When saying these prayers, keep a journal of the prayer and then allow time to listen to God's response. This is a time of reflection which is very important. During this time, God may lead you in an unexpected direction. He may even tell you to wait on something. Make notes during these times so that you can review them each time you pray. You just may find that a response you heard last week that did not make sense suddenly is now very clear.

Terri Savelle Foy writes in her book, *Dream It. Pin It. Live It.*, that a vision board "...is the expression of your dreams and goals in a tangible form so you have them in front of you for motivation and accountability." When we have our goals in front of us it becomes difficult to ignore them. It reminds us that we must work on these dreams on a daily basis. Each day we are either getting closer to or further away from our goals. Our vision boards, although beautiful to look at, are not pieces of artwork. If we merely hang them up and walk by them, we will start to ignore their importance. We will become clutter blind to it. If you feel the need, then change the location of your board from time to time. As long as you are seeing it daily, it does not matter if it is in the bedroom or the dining room. This is the reason we use our board. We state these goals out loud. We use it as one of our tools in prayer. We take down sections of it as we reach our goals. Our vision board is our action board. "And the Lord said to me, 'Write my answer on a billboard, large and clear, so that anyone can read it at a glance and rush to tell the others'." (Habakkuk 2:2 TLB) Writing it down, making it clear so that there is no doubt as to what is being sought.

"Furthermore, because we are united with Christ, we have received an inheritance from God, for he chose us in advance, and he makes everything work out according to his plan." (Ephesians 1:11 NLT) God has a plan for us. Our lives should be led as a form of worship to Him. Enjoy your life but keep a focus on your purpose.

Living the Dream

Take a glimpse into your future. You want to live the dream—your dream. When do you want this dream to become a reality? I would assume as soon as possible. Make your vision board today. Ask for God's guidance and pray over it. Listen for His response and then write it down. State aloud the dreams and goals from your vision board. You have the power to make these dreams a reality. Don't be afraid of your success. When is the best time to start this process? Now! Yes, there will be bumps in the road. Learn from these experiences. If you begin to work on your dreams immediately, you will give yourself the time needed for these life lessons along the way. You will learn and hopefully meet people, some like-minded and maybe some very different from you, whom you can learn from. If not now, when?

Your Turn:

Find photos representing three of your goals for this year. (You are not limited to just one picture per goal.) They should represent what that goal looks like for you. If you find better pictures later, then feel free to swap them out.

Goal (write it out)

#1:_____

_____

Target date:_____

Pictures you chose: _____

#2:_____

_____

Target date:_____

Pictures you chose: _____

#3:_____

_____

Target date:_____

Pictures you chose: _____

"Create a life you don't need a vacation from."

- Unknown

Chapter 6

Setting Goals: Turning Your Dreams Into Reality

Some people would consider themselves very goal-oriented. Another way of stating this would be to say that they are ambitious. For other people, merely the mention of setting goals causes them to roll their eyes and look away. Basically, we all want to be happy. For most people, this equates to similar desires such as a great paying and fulfilling career, a nice home, a loving family, and a killer bod. When you ask most people if they have goals, they will tell you "Yes" and many can actually state them to you. Or at least they think they are telling you their goals. What most people have, however, are merely wishes.

Wishes, Dreams, and Hopes

Many people use the terms goals, wishes, dreams, and hopes as synonyms thinking that these terms can be used interchangeably. Don't worry, I did too. In generalized conversation, this is okay as long as you know that there actually is a difference. Wishes, dreams, and hopes are passive. You are wishing, dreaming, and hoping that something will happen. The only effort being put forth is your mind thinking about it. As a matter of fact, you do not even have to be the one who came up with the idea. Some friends are talking, and one is telling you about the house they just bought. "Wow", you think, "I wish I had a brand-new house.", and that is where it ends. You have the desire for a new house but have no plans to put in any effort. As if some rich person was listening and would grant your wish and buy that new house for you. Don't feel bad, contemporary media is one of the culprits fostering this mentality. Watch any home improvement show and you can see a humble person who is blessed with a house, usually a fixer-upper that has been restored. (After all, this is the real reason for the televised program, which sponsors are paying good money to create.) Oh, and the fully restored house is complete with furniture that just happens to match their style. I grew up watching fairy tale-type television that always had the woman being rescued by her Prince Charming. Many women still live with this type of mindset, dreaming that someone will come to the rescue. After all, when we were children, our parents came to the rescue. Maybe for you, it was a grandparent who slid you some cash that really helped you out at the time. The problem is that slipping someone's money to buy ice cream is one thing but buying someone a house? Good luck! Here's something else to consider—would you even be able to afford a house if it were given to you? Could you afford the property taxes and upkeep? When the prince rescues the woman and they live happily ever after, what does that look like? Hmm, they never tell us because it is time for the credits and new commercials before the next movie. Maybe you come from a background in which wishing for that new house is where it ends. You have never had anyone on your side who had the resources to help you and therefore you and your family always did without. Dreams are all you had. When I was working on my graduate degree in social work, I remember one of my instructors talking to the class about the mindsets of our future clients. He informed us that we may be puzzled when conducting our home visits. He discussed his clients and how they had complete cable packages. Yes, cable! (I know I am dating myself here but just go with it, I am trying to make a point). They didn't have money to pay both the water and the cable bill. Regardless of their financial situation, that cable was going to stay on! It didn't seem to make sense. These people were of the mindset that since they were unable to pay all their bills, they would pay the ones which provided the most gratification. Apparently watching television was prioritized over bathing! They chose the short-term action which would give them the most enjoyment, for a time. It is the mentality of the poor. This is not the mentality that you want to take because it will not take you anywhere. There are sacrifices you must make now so that you can have a brighter future. One of the issues with the poverty mentality is an inability to see into the future because there are no examples of it that can be used as a reference. It is human nature to look at our past experiences and base decisions upon what we have seen work and not work for us. This is the reason for examining our life and life choices. Make note of what has worked and what has not worked for you as well as things that you have not even tried.

Wishes, dreams, and hopes may provide us with some comfort but they are not reality. Yes, I am sure you can tell me stories of how someone had their dream come true by having another person grant their wish but face reality, this is very rare. It is only on television that I have seen the rich uncle swoop in and save the day. Don't waste your life waiting for that wish to come true, take control and make it a reality for yourself.

> **Think About It:**
> If you could choose one of your goals which would have the greatest impact of your life, what would that goal be?

Prioritizing Your Goals

If you could choose a goal that, once achieved, would have the biggest impact on your life, what would that goal be? This is your nucleus goal. This achieved goal will positively influence other areas of your life. Prioritize your top three goals. Do something, however small it may be, to work towards these goals each day. Review your reasons for choosing these as your goals. Ask yourself "Why?" Why do you want to lose twenty pounds? What benefits would it provide? How will it impact your life? Perhaps your goal is to take your family on a big vacation. This can have a positive impact on your family cohesiveness. For each person and each goal, the response will be different. Remember these are personal goals you have set for yourself. They are not meant to impress anyone. Your goals must have meaning to you. You must create ownership to these goals.

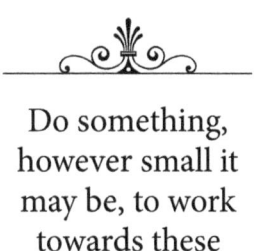

> Do something, however small it may be, to work towards these goals each day.

Hierarchy of Needs

Abraham Maslow was an American psychologist known best for his hierarchy of needs "A theory of psychological health predicated on fulfilling innate human needs in priority, culminating in self-actualization". If a person is having difficulty making ends meet, then it is difficult to focus on higher-level tasks. Ask yourself if you have basic needs that require tending to before reaching higher. Perhaps you have big goals, but your financial struggles keep getting in the way. Does that mean that you just forget about those goals? No! Does it mean that you lower your expectations? No! What it does mean, however, is that you will need to break that big goal into much smaller tasks. Your friend may have a goal of a job promotion while your mini-goal at this point is finding a scholarship to help pay for college classes. This is perfectly okay. You do not need to explain yourself to anyone. Be persistent. Your time will come.

Prayers

When writing out your goals, be sure to ask the Lord for guidance. As Christians, we want to work on goals that are in alignment with God's will. Our goals should not be too easy. They should stretch us. They should require assistance from the Lord. "So be careful how you live. Don't live like fools, but like those who are wise. Make the most of every opportunity in these evil days. Don't act thoughtlessly, but understand what the Lord wants you to do." (Ephesians 5:15-17 NLT) We need to be thoughtful in the actions we take and maximize our opportunities. Yes, there will be opportunities. This scripture reminds us to be intentional.

Goals and Personal Ownership

Have you ever seen the television show Hoarders? In this show, we see the hoarding person. This person is usually someone who has experienced some sort of trauma that has catapulted them into hoarding behavior. Then we are shown the friends or family members. These people are horrified by the living conditions that the hoarder is putting themself through. The friends and family make statements to the effect that they could help the person easily by just going into the house and throwing everything away. This is the point where the psychologist chimes in by educating the loved ones on how hoarding goes beyond the accumulation of belongings. It is the hoarder themself who must go through the procedures involved in decluttering. They must acknowledge and address their psychological issues before they can undertake the physical clutter and purge it. This process leads to releasing themselves from the internal prison they have created. This is one of those areas in which we cannot delegate tasks, the person must do it for themselves.

The show has discussed instances where others decluttered for their loved ones only to have that person create new clutter. Why? They did not deal with their hoarding issues. "How does this apply to me?" you may ask. "I am not a hoarder." "I do not feel the need to go through psychotherapy just to get my dream job!" Although as a social worker, I feel that everyone can benefit from counseling, I do agree that you do not have to be perfect to reach your dreams. You are, however, the only one who can achieve your dreams. You cannot delegate this.

If you want to lose twenty pounds, it is you who must reduce your caloric intake and exercise. No one can do this for you. Sure, you can have help along the way. After all, no one accomplishes success alone. There are people who can give you breaks along your journey and those who provide emotional encouragement is how you take advantage of this assistance and use it to propel you to success that matters. Reflect upon your past accomplishments. Is it not those accomplishments that required the most work on your part that meant the most to you? Once in a while, we do stumble upon a great break but for the most part, we must earn it ourselves. I prefer to think of it like getting a car. Would you rather work for that car and get exactly what you want within a year or wait five years and have a car given to you that is not exactly what you want? I have no intention of insulting anyone here, but if you choose the latter then you have a poverty mentality. Do not waste your life waiting for someone else to do the

You do not have to be perfect to reach your dreams.

work so that you can get their crumbs. Why purposely be the recipient of charity when you can be the giver? "Suppose one of you wants to build a tower. Won't you first sit down and estimate the cost to see if you have enough money to complete it?" (Luke 14:28 NIV) We need to strategize.

Is It in Your Control?

I love educational goals. The reason I love them so much is that they are straightforward. Once you have your major decided and are enrolled in a university there is a guide that tells you exactly what courses you need to take to obtain your degree. Sure, there are a few electives, and of course, there are always the trials involved with a difficult class or temperamental professor, but the process is straightforward. Complete A, B, C, and D and you have earned yourself a college degree. Ahh, if all goals had such a straightforward process. Many times, you may find yourself having a goal with which you have or feel that you have no control over. For example, you may have a goal of having children. To a great extent, much of this goal is out of your control. For instance, if you are single then you are going to need a partner who buys into this goal of yours. Once you have navigated this obstacle then there are physical considerations of whether or not you are fertile. There are things you can do physically to increase your odds and there are also options of non-biological parenting such as adoption. Many single people have a goal of getting married. Once again, there is a challenge here in which you are dependent upon another person being willing and appropriate to marry.

Depending on another person to be a part of your goal is a scary process and can lead to disappointment. This is where you must take serious consideration to reframing your goals. If your goal is to have children (and this is a great goal) then be specific. Do you want to only have children with a specific person, or by a certain age? Is it only important to you if it is your biological child? When your goal involves a specific person to be a part of it you will need a contingency plan. You cannot control other people therefore it is not 100% in your control to meet your goal. You need to be flexible. Maybe adoption or foster care can be possible options. If you want to get married, you will need to have clear expectations of the type of person you want to marry. What if you cannot meet someone who embodies these criteria? Do you change your criteria? Do you have a timeline in which to marry? Would you rather remain single instead of compromising your criteria for a spouse? This contingency plan can only be made by you. Only you know the importance of this goal. Just be aware of the areas within your goal attainment that may be out of your control such as other people and health impairments. Maybe it is specific, such as a particular job that you want. If there are no positions, then you need to decide if you are willing to relocate for your career or to increase your skills while waiting for a position. If you choose to wait, be sure that you have a time frame set up. Otherwise waiting may turn out to be a goal that is never realized.

While watching *Dancing with the Stars* one evening, I saw an interesting interview with Drew Scott. He stated he always had a desire to be a famous actor. Despite his efforts, he was unable to attain his dream. He recalled his father giving him some great advice, telling him "If someone ever says you can't do something, find five ways to do it." Drew continued on to state that he learned "There's not just one way to achieve a goal." He responded to this by taking something he was good at and parlaying it into a reality show. The rest is television history. He learned the importance of thinking outside the box and not allowing obstacles to derail his progress toward his dreams and goals. Life does not always turn out according to our plans. Sometimes it turns out better. "Commit your actions to the LORD, and your plans will succeed." (Proverbs 16: NLT) We need to have a plan.

SMART Goals

Is establishing a goal good enough? No, it is not. Your goal must be written out. In writing out these goals you are engaging in self-accountability. There is a famous study conducted by Harvard University. This study was performed from 1979–1989 on MBA graduates. In this study, the graduates were asked if they had clearly written goals with plans to carry out the goal. Of those studied, in 1979, only 3% of the graduates had clearly written goals. Another 13% had established goals, but not in writing. The remaining 84% had no established goals. Ten years later, in 1989, these graduates were examined. It was discovered that the 3% who had clearly written goals were earning ten times more money than those who had not written out their goals.

Pens and paper are inexpensive. Go out and get some! It will be worth it! Once we decide to write out our goals, we need to ensure we write them out correctly. In 1981, George T. Doran provided us with a framework for properly addressing our goals. Perhaps you are familiar with his concept represented by the SMART acronym. We need to write our goals in the format of a SMART goal. I'm sure that you may have already heard of making a goal SMART but let me guide you through the SMART technique as I know it

S—Specific
M—Measurable
A—Achievable
R—Relevant
T—Time Based

Specific: Be specific in describing what you want. Perhaps you want to increase your social life. What does that look like for you? Does it mean having social events to attend? Does it mean having more friends? For each person, this will look different.

Measurable: There needs to be a method to measure what you want. For instance, if you want to increase your social circle you may say that you want two friends, as evidenced by people that you can text on the weekend to ask to hang out. The key term here is "as evidenced by". In social work, when writing my progress notes I would frequently use this term. It would go something like this:

The patient appeared distraught, as evidenced by her crying.

This translates to reporting that my interpretation of the patient being distraught was seeing the patient cry. It allows for various interpretations. Just because a person cries does not mean the person is distraught. A person can also cry tears of happiness. In the case of your goals, just because you can call a person does not mean they are your friend, but it is how you are defining a friend. This measurable quality will differ for each person. It should be a measure that could be seen by others. In this example, having two friends is the goal, and the definition of a friend, in this case, is determined by the fact that they could be texted for possible social outings on the weekend. For others, it may look different such as having someone to talk to on the phone.

Achievable: This needs to be an achievable goal. Although your goals should involve hard work and prayer, they should fall into the category of being probable not merely possible. You want a goal that stretches you emotionally, not one that will leave you feeling discouraged.

Relevant: Your goal should be relevant, in other words, it needs to be applicable to your lifestyle. If you are a hermit, then making friends may not be relevant to you. If you are moving to a new city then it is very relevant to have a goal of making new friends.

Time based: To solidify your goal you must make this time-based. Each goal should have a target date. How long do you want to take to make new friends? Maybe you moved to a new city during the summer, then setting a goal to make friends by Labor Day would set this to be an achievable goal.

Based on the SMART acronym, this goal would be written as:

> *"I want to make two friends, as evidenced by people that I can text on the weekend to ask to hang out, by Labor Day."*

Now that we know what a SMART goal is, the question becomes "Why do we need smart goals?" How do SMART goals relate to you achieving your goals? A SMART goal allows us a manner in which to measure our progress toward our goals. It allows us to know when we have crossed the finish line.

Many times people get to the end of their goal process, when their goal is within their reach, they simply end the process. They say that it is "good enough" and give up. It is as if they have no energy left at the end of the journey. It is when we are towards the attainment of our goals that we often feel the most discouraged. Why is this? This is because we are tired, we have put in the hard work and most probably had to overcome obstacles. I like to compare this to running a marathon. When you see the runners finish the race, do they look as fresh as when they started? Of course not, they are sweaty and tired. After they finish and get a little rest in, however, you will find that they are pleased they followed through with the process. Making a SMART goal helps to keep you on track. When working on goals we will have setbacks. Life gets messy, people get tired. Creating goals using the SMART technique helps keep us focused on our goals. It will help you to maintain momentum while providing you with appropriate compromises to make in the event that things do not go according to plan, and you must respond quickly.

When making a SMART goal you cannot be vague. Quite the opposite, you must be as specific as possible. It should be able to be measured by someone other than the person setting the goal. It is a goal that has clarity. Therefore, you have no doubt as to where you are aiming. Like driving a car with clean windows!

Deadlines and Target Dates

Deadlines and target dates provide us with a sense of accountability. What is the difference between a deadline and a target date? As I stated in my vision board chapter, "A goal is a dream with a deadline." I am not sure I like the concept of a deadline. Get married by age forty or what? Give up, become a spinster? To me, deadlines involve negative consequences. For instance, with employment having a deadline implies that if you do not meet the goal by a specific date then you will cease to be compensated financially. In your personal life, I prefer to set these limits by referring to them as target dates, in other words, dates to aim toward. Some goals, however, will require a deadline. For example, if you wish to marry and start a family, a common deadline of age forty to accomplish this task can be set. If you do not meet the deadline, you can employ the contingency plan of starting a family on your own, through foster care or adoption.

Each day you are either moving closer to or further away from attaining your goals. I realize that some goal activities may only require action on a weekly basis therefore, each week you need to conduct an assessment so that the month does not get away from you. Set target dates in order to provide motivation to keep going rather than delaying your goals. You must have a sense of urgency when it comes to working on these goals. What happens if you set a target date and fail to complete your goal by that date? Do you give up? No! You extend the date. Does this mean that you have failed? No! For example, delays happen all the time in home construction. If your new house was scheduled to be completed in March but then you were informed that there would be a six-week delay, would you change your mind about buying it? Of course not, these delays are quite common. Then why would you consider giving up on your dreams if they became delayed? Do not take a break at this point. I know it can feel defeating to not make a goal within a certain timeframe, but this is not an excuse to give up on your goal. You may have to alter the route that it takes to get there or accept the fact that it may take longer than you anticipated, but do not give up. Review your timeline for attaining this goal and set a new and realistic target date. These are your goals. Never give up on yourself!

Motivation

Many people give up on their dreams when they find that it takes work to attain them. Most people will set small goals, which they know they can achieve. Setting and achieving a small goal can be great for building self-confidence. It is good to have a variety of large and small goals. This is the reason that placing smaller goals on your vision board is important. It's great to dream huge dreams. Try to build in motivators to keep you going along the way. A good example of this is with weight loss goals. Notice I chose a goal that could be easily measured. Let's say your goal is to lose twenty pounds. How long you take to accomplish this task depends on you. Are there obstacles such as parties and celebrations? What if you sprain your ankle and cannot exercise? This may set back your progress. These are your goals. You get to set your own pace. Maybe the pace you set is too slow and you lose motivation. This can even cause you to rationalize yourself out of your goal. How about setting incremental goals such as losing weight in five-pound increments? How about giving yourself some rewards along the way? For weight loss, it can be something like a bottle of perfume, a new pair of earrings, or a new book for every five pounds. It is okay to give yourself external rewards along the way as long as you do not make this a stopping point. Always ask the Lord to guide you along this process.

Regardless of how you feel about the process of goal setting, it is an important vehicle to use in getting you to the destination of attaining your dreams. The Lord put these desires in your heart. He wants you to fulfill your destiny. Design your life by creating your SMART goals, pray over them, and work on them daily. The effort you put into this will change your life and most probably the lives of others.

SMART Goal Worksheet

Today's Date: _____ Target Date: _____
Date of first action: _____

Specific—What specifically do you want to accomplish?
_____
_____

Measurable—How will you know when you have accomplished this goal?
_____
_____

What form of measurement will you use?
_____
_____

Are you able to measure your progress along the way? Yes / No

Achievable—Is this goal possible? Yes / No
Do you know someone who has accomplished this goal? Yes / No
Do you have the resources necessary in order to work on this goal? Yes / No

Relevant—How is this goal significant to your life?
_____
_____

Timely-What is your target date?

_____

SMART Goal:

_____

_____

_____

Potential Obstacles

_____

_____

_____

_____

_____

Resources

_____

_____

_____

_____

_____

Potential Solutions

_____

_____

_____

_____

_____

People to help

_____
_____
_____
_____
_____

Milestone Action Steps: What steps need to be taken to reach this goal?
Action: _____

Your Turn:

Complete your first three goals.

1. List your first 3 goals using the SMART format:

Goal #1

_____

_____

Goal #2

_____

_____

Goal #3

_____

_____

1. Read your goals aloud.
2. For the next 30 days, state your goals aloud and rewrite them.

Section III

Getting What You Want by Taking Charge

Dreaming. Setting goals. Envisioning your future. This entire process sounds enjoyable, but we don't want to just sit on the couch with a silly smile on our faces fantasizing about a perfect life. We want to go out there and make our dreams a reality. This will require work, sacrifice, and of course prayer.

In Section III, we will learn about getting what we want out of life by taking charge. We will discuss time management as well as how to overcome our fears, so we do not get stuck in our comfort zone. We will focus on seizing opportunities and living with intention.

Jesus my Savior,

We praise Your name and Your miraculous nature. Thank You for the sacrifices You have made for us. Thank You for the life we have as well as our free will. Please help us to be appreciative of the gifts You have given us. Help us to continue to trust in You as we go outside of our comfort zone in order to reach our full potential. We ask that You continue to guide us as we apply the principles of time management and intentional living from this section of the book.

Amen

"You will never find time for anything. If you want time, you must make it!"

- Charles Buxton

Chapter 7

Time Management: Taking Charge of Your Life

Time is what our life is made of. We cherish time with loved ones and wish away time during activities we despise. I have heard it said that the manner in which you manage your time is the same in which you manage your life. I think just about everyone has used the excuse "I just don't have the time". When we run into someone who seems to have it all together, we ask "Where do you find the time?" People often state how busy they are as if to brag. As if being super busy equates to having it all together. I have even heard people make reference to someone's accomplishment by stating things such as "Hmm, must have had a lot of time on their hands". Would that be considered a backhanded compliment or an outright stab in the back? Defining one's life according to time management? Interesting!

Where Does the Time Go?

If you have ever attended a high school graduation it is not uncommon to overhear a parent saying, "Where did the time go?" They talk of how quickly their little baby grew up and lament at how this child is now leaving the nest. "It seems like it was just yesterday that they were learning to ride a bicycle." We get nostalgic. Life does go by quickly, whether we appreciate those special little moments or not.

Do you ever get so busy with your days that before you realize it the week is gone? Maybe it's the end of the year and you are looking at those "resolutions" you set last New Year's Eve that somehow fell by the wayside. Don't worry, this happens to everyone. We often say that we have good intentions, but life gets in the way. The family vacation that never happened, the garage we were going to clear out to make room for the ping-pong table, the credit card we were going to pay off, everyone has good intentions. No one says they are looking forward to experiencing marital problems, health crises, or financial struggles, but it happens. We often get caught cleaning up situations that we did not plan for, thus sacrificing all the meaningful events if we are not careful.

Why Do We Need to Manage Our Time?

Life has a tendency to get away from us, yet we only have a limited amount of time here on Earth. It is imperative that we manage the time that we do have. A simple look at your environment can reveal the focus we have on time.

Clocks are not only used as decorative items displayed on our walls. There are time displays in our vehicles, our computers, and our ovens. Our cell phones have enabled us all to be synched in time. Despite being used to track our daily steps, our Smartwatches prominently display the current hour and minutes. I don't have to remind you how many clocks are in our lives. Twice a year during daylight savings we run around adjusting these clocks and changing their batteries. Although frequently stated by young women, we often hear the phrase "My clock is ticking". If time were not so important, why is it so ingrained in our culture? We need to remember that clocks are merely measurement tools and there certainly is no need to feel stressed by them.

Pacing our tasks through time management techniques can help us to reduce the stress we may feel with so many competing demands in our lives. There are many benefits to time management practices such as increased productivity at work, improvement in the quality of our relationships, goal attainment, increased leisure time as well as increased confidence and self-discipline. Managing our time can help us to complete the tasks that need to be accomplished and allow us the opportunity to be with our families and pursue our personal interests.

The Gift of Time

I believe many of us were put to the test when the COVID pandemic struck. Suddenly, there were lockdowns, and we were confined to our homes. Some people used this time to get closer to their families, declutter and spruce up their homes, write books and songs, and get serious about their workouts. Others, however, wound up in divorce court, shopped way too much online, and most gained weight. We have long heard of the "freshman fifteen", well there is now the "COVID twenty". Clearly, we were given the gift of time, not really in the manner we would have wanted to receive it, but nonetheless, we had more time to investigate personal interests. Some used the time wisely while others whittled it away. Let's not use time as an excuse for not fulfilling those dreams. According to TD Jakes in his book *Destiny*, "The issue is not time or that you are busy, but whether the actions and activities that consume your time are leading to your destiny." How you spend your time is a choice you make. Are you being productive or just busy? Time will pass either way. Make sure you are not wasting it.

> Are you being productive or just busy?

How Do We Manage Our Time?

We know managing our time is important but with so many competing demands in life, how do we begin the process of time management? Effectively managing our time involves setting priorities, and then avoiding anything that is not in alignment with those priorities. One must create a plan for task completion as well as goal attainment.

Procrastination

When people speak of time management, its evil cousin procrastination is usually brought up. Everyone procrastinates, it is inevitable. Many times, it is because we have tasks to complete that are not fun. Sometimes, it is due to having a series of steps involved in a project or involving collaboration with others which can delay one's progress. To conquer those tasks, we should act with a sense of urgency. Just get things done so that you can move on to more desirable tasks. Think about the times you worried for hours over an undesirable task that once completed, turned out to only take a matter of minutes. Acting with a sense of urgency could have eliminated hours of stress.

If we do choose to procrastinate, we should use this procrastination as a tool. Procrastination can, when used strategically, be used to our benefit. In his book, *Eat That Frog!*, Brian Tracy acknowledges we are often overwhelmed with tasks and therefore cannot do everything. He suggests we should "...procrastinate on low-value activities.", reporting we need to "...eliminate those activities that don't make much of a contribution to your life..." If we are selective with what we choose to work on, we will have enough time to do the few things that really matter in our lives. Notice this form of procrastination only works when we have identified our priorities.

Think About It:
Does how you spend your time reflect your priorities?

Priorities

Everyone has setbacks: financial crises, health problems, drama at the office, issues with relatives, the list can go on and on. We tell our family we will be home by six and wouldn't you know it, the computer goes down right before you were to send the end-of-the-day report and now you must stay until it is complete. These things happen and we often feel we have no choice but to respond to it. Many of us spend our entire days handling these unforeseen problems and then have no time left to get our job duties completed. It is not uncommon to arrive at work with a to-do list and then leave for the day with not only an incomplete list but having more piled on to it.

During the day there are urgent tasks and important duties. An important duty for a teacher would be entering grades into the computer to generate report cards by the due date. Getting a report card entered is a necessary duty and one for which teachers are hired to complete. Imagine that one of the students had a meltdown towards the end of the school day. Helping a child in crisis would be an urgent task for a teacher. It would be totally irresponsible for the teacher to not take care of the child who is having a meltdown. The report card is the job duty, which is important, and the meltdown situation is the urgent task. Although urgent tasks may occur at your job, you would be surprised at how many employers turn a blind eye to this and continue to demand your important duties be completed. Many employers may even state that dealing with these emergencies is an excuse for not completing your work. This is the reason simple tasks take so long. You think you are just going to walk to the copy room and make a couple of copies. The copy machine jams. You must stop to fix it. In the process you encounter coworkers who either waste your time with chatter or worse yet, ask something of you, thus adding more to your plate. Yes, we must deal with urgent tasks, but we still must attend to our important duties.

It is important to acknowledge that priorities often change as our circumstances change. This is the reason we must evaluate our lives consistently. This is similar to weighing yourself regularly. Perhaps you have heard, or even experienced, the following scenario: You wear casual clothes for a while, (think COVID and yoga pants!), then one day there is a need to wear more formal clothing. You go to your closet and pull out your trusty old black slacks. You put them on and to your horror, they are very tight. You then pull out the scale, blow off the dust, and weigh yourself. Whoa! There is a ten-pound weight gain. You knew you put on a little weight, but thought it was only a pound or two. Somehow your weight got away from you. You did not realize it because you were not monitoring it. This probably happened so slowly that you didn't realize it until you tried on the pants. As much as you may hate your scale, it is a very quick and easy way to evaluate your weight status.

A number on a scale or in a bank account is objective. Taking an evaluation of other areas of your life such as your relationships is subjective, and you will therefore need to put increased effort into this type of evaluation. If you decide you want a happy marriage, then you need to define what a happy marriage looks like to both you and your spouse. In relationships, we often think in terms of the feelings we experience when we are with others. Having feelings such as safety, love, awkwardness, or uneasiness may come to mind when thinking of specific relationships. Evaluate your relationships frequently to determine if they are of the quality level which you intend them to be. Many times, our daily life, actions will impact our relationships and before we realize it, our relationships are out of whack. If you find that a particular relationship needs more attention, then you can shift your weekly priorities to accommodate working on this.

Each time you conduct a self-evaluation, ask yourself to identify your priorities. Be honest because this evaluation is only for you. If your priority is your career that is okay. Most people will say their relationships are a priority in their lives, but their actions do not reflect this. Some people may be in relationships with others out of convenience, fear of being alone, or merely for companionship, and thus have a take-it or leave-it mentality regarding the person. If your priority really is your relationships, make sure these people can feel that priority. Of course, you must attend to your job because you need to survive financially but ensure, however, that you know how to set boundaries while in the workplace. We set boundaries at work when we decline additional duties, leave by five, or even when we refuse to work through lunch. We set boundaries in a relationship when we start dinner without that person when they are late or end a conversation if the person becomes disrespectful.

Reactive versus Proactive

Are you being reactive or proactive in your life? If you are being reactive you are waiting for things to happen and then responding to it. If you are being proactive then you are making things happen. When we spend time on activities we are making a choice. We are choosing one activity over another. When you choose to stay late at work, you are choosing work over family time. Make certain when you do this, that it aligns with your personal values and is not merely a habit which has been formed.

"For a man does not know his time. Like fish that are taken in an evil net, and like birds that are caught in a snare, so the children of man are snared at an evil time when it suddenly falls upon them." (Ecclesiastes 9:12 ESV) This reminds me that in life, bad things will happen. We need to anticipate such things occurring. There will be rainy days, the flu, and broken relationships. We need to create a contingency plan for life. If we fail to create such a plan, we will be responding to these events in a reactive manner. If we create this contingency plan, then we are behaving in a proactive manner.

Distractions

Do you waste time? We all waste time at some point and some waste more time than others. I think you are already aware of the major time wasters: television, gaming, social media, and gossiping at work. Do you continue to engage in these activities? Are you cognizant of these actions? Just because you spend time on social media does not mean that you are wasting your life away. Sometimes we need a two-minute break. Social media, used correctly, can be an excellent networking tool for both business and social endeavors. A little television at the end of the day to relax and garnish some laughter is a great stress reliever and a bonus if watched with the family, prompting quality discussions. Remember, all work and no play equals no life.

If you experience distractions which hinder your ability to accomplish important tasks, then you need to take charge of this. Your employer, most likely, hired you to complete specific tasks and probably "other duties as assigned". Getting your tasks completed may involve getting to the office early or perhaps taking work home where coworkers won't interrupt you. Maybe the crises you are dealing with are at home, such as coping with a child who has temper tantrums. Your goal of a relaxing family dinner is ruined when you spend the evening dealing with unprovoked outbursts. Taking time out to evaluate the family dynamics here is crucial so that you do not burn out as a parent.

The key question to ask yourself is whether you are controlling your time or is time controlling you. Here's an example: shopping. A man says he needs a pair of jeans. He goes to the store, heads straight to the western wear section, chooses a pair of jeans, tries them on and then purchases them, gets back in his truck, and goes about his day. A woman, however, will browse the sections of the store on the way to the jeans area, choose several different styles, try them on, inquire about store discounts, and then maybe purchase, or decide to choose another store to browse. On the way out of the store, she will window shop and perhaps even come home with another outfit, purse or pair of shoes. Either manner of shopping is fine, as long as you are honest with yourself about how long the process should take. For me, spending that extra time at the mall is enjoyable and "fills my cup", so I do not consider it a time waster at all.

A Time for Rest

What about lying around the house doing nothing, should we do this? Yes, we should! The Bible talks about the Sabbath day. It is great to be productive but at a certain point, we will start to make mistakes if we just keep pushing on to work. In the social service field, I observed many counselors come into an agency full of energy and ready to make a difference. They filled in when others were out sick, worked overtime, bought items for the agency with their own money, and put their all into the position. I also observed these same employees leaving the agency as fast as they entered. They burned themselves out. Don't get me wrong, I loved the enthusiasm of these co-workers, but it seemed as though they put every ounce of their energy into the agency and then left nothing for themselves. You just can't maintain that pace without breaking. It's like a person on an overly strict workout routine. They go for a while without any deviation from a rigid routine and then wind up either sustaining an injury or just quitting the workout altogether. At some point you need to be a taker: take breaks as needed, take a duty-free lunch, take a text break to check in on your significant other during the day, take the initiative to go to bed at a reasonable hour, you get the point. If you are spending so much energy on your responsibilities that you are skimping on meals and sleep, then it is time to re-evaluate those responsibilities. Many people will push you until you either set a boundary with them or push back.

If you feel that time has been getting away from you, take three days to track your activities in thirty-minute increments. Yes, I said thirty-minute increments. Jot down the main activity you engage in both at home and work. Do not use "miscellaneous" in your documentation. Three days should be sufficient to discover where your time is going. You may find that the mere process of documenting your time causes you to be more conscientious about how you utilize time. It can also bring to light how much time is wasted in terms of minutes. Most of the time we waste is not necessarily the hours but those minutes here and there that simply accumulate. Just like using your credit card for a few dollars here and there, it all adds up.

Interference from the Enemy

Even the best-laid plans can fail. As much as I do not like to think about it, the devil does interfere in our lives. Sometimes, we experience delays or roadblocks in working towards attaining our goals. At other times, we are kept so busy that we do not have time for the important things. Often, when feeling overwhelmed by the daily flow of life, people will drop items off their schedule because there is simply no time left. Be honest with yourself here—have you ever missed a church service because something else was going on? What about prayer time with God? I think we can all relate to the end-of-day prayer time where we were so tired that we fell asleep. We are human, thus, we are all guilty of this. What appears to be an innocent scheduling issue may in actuality be the devil trying to interfere. Our time with the Lord should always be our top priority.

Seasons

Nothing lasts forever, everything is temporary. Good times do not last forever but neither do the bad times. Maybe you are going through a rough season, being a single mom, taking care of aging parents, or dealing with a health crisis. Living your best life does not feel like an option to you during this time. I get it. I've been there. Regardless of how difficult it may feel, remember that your children continue to grow, your parents continue to age, and regardless of how little time you have, your health must be addressed. You may feel as though your time is not your own right now, but it will come back to you. Remind yourself that being a parent is a choice, taking care of your parents is a privilege, and leading a healthy lifestyle is crucial because, without your health, it is difficult to live your best life. Just as the seasons change, so will this time in your life.

In this life, we will have opportunities to share our love of Christ. We need to seize all these opportunities. "Make the most of your chances to tell others the Good news. Be wise in all your contacts with them." (Colossians 4:5 TLB) This reminds me of my mother-in-law's funeral sermon. The pastor spoke of our limited time on earth to share the Word of God, and that once we die, our fate is sealed and then it is too late. He stated that my mother-in-law's fate was now set but we still had the opportunity to spread the word. You never know when it will be too late. Regardless of what season you are currently in, do not allow opportunities to praise the Lord to pass you by.

Making a Plan

You have set your priorities and acknowledged how to avoid common distractions. Now it is time to make a plan. Get out your planner! What I love about my planner is being able to look at the entire year in a glance. Our daily plans have an impact on our week. Our weekly accomplishments have an impact on our month. We only have twelve months in a year. You know how time works, and you know that it is gone in the blink of an eye.

There is a powerful video online, that I am sure many have seen, of a demonstration by a professor. In this video, he places golf balls, pebbles, and sand into a jar. It is to symbolize life and the many demands we have on our time. The golf balls represented the most important tasks, the pebbles were the next important and the sand was the least important. The way to fit everything in the jar is to put the largest items in first and then the smaller items manage to wiggle their way in. The lesson being taught was that if you prioritize the important things, then the menial issues will fall into place. For example, would you miss a graduation service in order to complete your weekly grocery shopping?

Look at your planner and strategize how you will break down your vision board goals to meet your target dates. Every day you should be doing something to work on at least one of your goals, no matter how small that task may be. Every day we must spend time with God. Does it seem weird to schedule time for God? It shouldn't. Some days it may be a church service or life group while others it is Bible reading. What do you think church service times are? You should already have your Sunday service time scheduled into your week. Church service is an appointment with God. This one-hour commitment, however, is not enough for your week. I like to refer to it as my formal time with the Lord, guided by my pastor. You also will need to schedule your praise and worship, Bible reading, and prayer time. I know that may sound like a lot, but God is always with us. Our prayer time can be as simple as talking to God during our daily drive to work. Ideally, however, it should be distraction-free. We want to be available to hear whatever the Lord chooses to reveal to us.

> Every day we must spend time with God.

You Are Only Young Once

As much as spontaneity is praised, I do believe that we must plan out things in our lives. Time is the great equalizer. We all have the same number of hours in our day. Unfortunately, not everyone has the same number of years left. For this reason, taking care of your health should be a top priority. Even with health as a significant issue, there is no guarantee as to how many years you have left. Consider the quality of life you desire. I have seen many people stricken with an illness that allows them to live many years but with a lack of quality of life.

We talk about our bucket lists. Many times, we feel that we have the rest of our lives to complete what is on this list. Have you done the math on this? For instance, we all tend to think that we will live to be one hundred. So, when we are fifty, we call ourselves middle-aged. I'm sorry to tell you but most people do not live to be one hundred. In fact, it is actually very rare. Even Betty White did not quite make it. As a general rule, take the age of your parents and grandparents. Who lived the longest? Was it a grandmother who lived to age ninety? Based on this, if you are fifty you have forty years left to live. If one of your bucket list items is to run a 10k, do you see yourself doing it at age ninety? Maybe if you are George Bush! At what age would you want to do this task so that you could fully enjoy it? How about quality time with a relative? Do you want to wait until your parents are in a retirement home before making time for them? Plan out these long-term items. Most planners have a section where you can view five years ahead. Use that feature and plan for long-term goals and priorities.

The Investment of Time

We should consider time as a commodity. Be careful to guard your time and not waste it on activities unrelated to your goals, ambitions, or loved ones. This will look different for each person. Sometimes you may find yourself working at a job you do not like but which represents a stepping stone to something better. These things will happen, it is called "Paying your dues". Sometimes you may spend time socializing with people you do not prefer but you do it for the sake of a loved one. This is not done in vain; it is considered an investment. Are you using time as an investment tool? You should. Every day you should be doing something to get closer to your goals. Setbacks are going to occur, but successful people consider setbacks as learning tools. If you are able to glean a lesson from the experience, then your effort is not wasted. If possible, delegate and outsource tasks that are not important to you. For example, you can do your own sewing alterations and if you enjoy sewing it can serve as a great source of satisfaction and pride. For myself, however, it is not how I want to spend my time. I choose to delegate this task and pay to have someone alter my clothing. It saves me not only the time and effort of doing something I despise but also the mental stress of its anticipation. I also feel good that I am helping someone to earn money by supporting their small business.

Remember that life gets in the way and there will be times that we need to tweak our plans. Don't just fall for the idea of having a busy week, because every week should be busy. You do not want to wake up one morning and find that life has passed you by. Think of this as a car ride. You wouldn't start driving if you hadn't first decided where you were going. You would decide on a destination before pulling out of the driveway. Then suppose you encountered some road construction involving a detour. Would you just turn around and go back home? Of course not. If there was a great deal of construction, you may not even have the option to turn back. The same is true with life. Events happen that change us, whether we ask for it or not. The only true constant in life is change.

Perfectionism

One issue that often deters people from completing tasks is that of perfectionism. Some people are simply not able to finish projects due to the constant nagging feeling something is not perfect or does not look the way they had originally envisioned. This can be difficult because you want to maintain your standards. At a certain point, however, you may need to realize that not everything will turn out in the manner of your original intent. It is great to maintain these standards but is also okay to not be perfect. How much time do you have to complete your project? Does the completion of this project have any bearing on future projects? You certainly do not want your perfectionism on one goal or project to hinder any future projects. Evaluate the situation and make a clear decision as to when to finalize your project.

Working on Goals

"Teach us to number our days, that we may gain a heart of wisdom." (Psalm 90:12 NIV) When we think of how limited our time is on any task, it makes us work harder and respect that time. When planning out your goals, assign a target date to it. For instance, you may have a goal of a big family vacation. You want to be able to carry out this plan while the kids are still living at home. Perhaps education is your goal. You want to follow up on this goal as soon as feasible so that you can reap as many benefits from it as possible. Your goals will be as unique as you are. Make sure that you give yourself the proper amount of time to attain them. You are the steward of the time the Lord has given you. Use it wisely.

Your Turn:

Look at the items you have prioritized as first and second on your list of goals. Schedule time to work on these goals and list the specific task you will be doing.

Goal #1: _____

Day of week: _____ Time: _____
Task to be accomplished:
_____

Goal #2: _____

Day of week: _____ Time: _____

Task to be accomplished:
_____

How much time have you allocated for your goals this week?
_____

Scheduled church service time: _____

Scheduled prayer time: _____

"Intentional living is the art of making our own choices before others' choices make us."

- Richie Norton

Chapter 8

Living with Intention: Seizing Opportunities

Most people consider flexibility a positive trait. Awakening with good intentions and high hopes, they go about their lives seeing where each day leads them. Flexibility is a great trait to possess. However, God did not provide our lives for us to respond like little silver balls in a pinball machine, just reacting to situations thrown at us. It is easy to be reactive, most of the time we act out of reflex. This book is not about being reactive. It is about being proactive in our lives. It is about living our lives in an intentional manner so we can serve the Lord.

Going Through the Motions

I have, more times than I would like to admit, gone through my day just dragging, going through the daily motions. I know I have not been the only one. I will tell you this, however, when I hear a co-worker or friend who is dragging through the day, just like me, reporting anything to the idea of "getting this over with" or doing something to "kill time"–it drives me bonkers. I have no intention of killing time. Till when? Life is precious and tomorrow is not guaranteed. Why would a person ever want to kill time? We should live each day as if it is our last. I know this is much easier said than done. If we were to live each day as if it were our last, we may become negligent in handling our obligations and therefore the functioning of our lives would suffer. This could also have a negative impact on the lives of others. Let's face it, there are a lot of aspects of adult life that are not fun. We can't have cake for dinner every night. (Trust me I've tried it and my thighs rebelled!) Take care of those obligations and keep your eyes and ears open. There may be a friend or family member who needs to spend time with you and hear your encouraging words. This may be your last day to see that person. Cherish these times together.

I love the movie Hitch with Will Smith. It's about a man who had challenges in the romance department of his life. To conquer these challenges, he designs a strategy for making women fall in love with their admirers. One of the things I love about the movie is that Hitch doesn't keep his winning strategy to himself. He develops a business and helps other forlorn men to obtain the love of the women they desire. He was not only an entrepreneur but helped others in the process. My favorite line from this movie is when Hitch says, "Begin each day as if it were on purpose." How many of us can say we do this? Do you wake up with an intention for each day?

I enjoy taking yoga classes. I like the physical benefits as well as how relaxed I feel afterward. During most of these classes, the instructor will ask the participants to set an intention for their yoga practice during the following hour. At first, it threw me for a loop. I hadn't thought about an intention for that particular session. My intention was just to go to the gym and take a class. Now, I enter the class and set an intention for that hour. Sometimes it is to improve flexibility in a certain area, other times it may be to increase balance and many times it is to develop a sense of calmness. I would have never started making an intention for my yoga class had it not been brought to my attention.

What Does it Mean to Live Your Life with Intention?

Living your life with intention means that of the multitude of decisions you make in a day, you are being purposeful with your choices. Since there are innumerable decisions to be made each day, most of our daily choices are made out of habit. It would be impossible to think through every single decision that you need to make each day. Some people have so many daily decisions that they experience decision fatigue. We often must rely on our habits to make these daily decisions. According to James Clear in his book *Atomic Habits,* "Habits are mental shortcuts learned from experience."

We make decisions all the time. When I was in college, I took a class on decisions. Yes, for an entire semester, we were lectured on decision-making. We learned that there are both minor and major decisions. Some of these decisions are simple and have only a minor impact upon our lives and others have long-term consequences. Certainly, you would not treat the decisions of what to fix for dinner and whether to have children in the same manner. Merely the act of making a decision is significant because not making a decision is actually a decision.

Even when we are amiss the consequences of our behaviors, we have a choice in terms of our attitude and how we approach our new situation. How is your attitude? Can you see beyond the immediate circumstances and look to the big picture? Sometimes we need to reframe our situation. The act of reframing involves looking at our circumstances from a different point of view. It often results in us appreciating a situation or person that we have taken for granted.

What are you living for today? Why did God give you this day? Not every day will be monumental. Many of our days are building blocks as we make our climb to the top of the mountain of success. Most of the conversations and time we spend with others are seeds being planted that will bloom in the future. In some way, every day, however small, we should make our actions count.

We need to live a life of intentionality. Even our social lives should be conducted with intention. If you are single, you should be placing yourself in an environment abundant with like-minded singles. If you are married, you should be focusing on nurturing your marriage. Everyone should be trying to create happy memories. Regardless of your particular circumstances, you should be seeking to make a difference in this world.

At this point, you may be feeling a little pressured. If you are trying to make the most of every minute of your life and have every encounter with another human being to contain meaning, it can be stressful. Anxiety can even develop. It is okay to rest and to decline social invitations. Not every opportunity presented to you needs to be accepted. Remember that just because you *can* do something does not mean that you *should* do something. The key is balance. This is the reason you need to do a monthly self-evaluation. Are you accepting so many invitations that you feel overwhelmed? In an effort to be there for everyone, is your attitude suffering? If you conduct activities with a poor attitude, then it is defeating your purpose, you will be working against yourself. Are you at the other end of the spectrum where you are turning down most of the invitations you receive and getting a little too comfy on that couch?

> Just because you *can* do something does not mean that you *should* do something.

One approach to take when trying to live intentionally is to embrace mindfulness. According to Witkiewitz, Roos, Dharmakaya, Colgan, and Bowen, in their text *Mindfulness*, from a therapeutic standpoint mindfulness is "...developing a clear awareness of one's present internal or personal experiences, including thoughts, emotions, sensations, and behaviors, as well as attention to perceptions of elements in the surrounding environment, such as sights and sounds" In simple terms this means taking an assessment of both your external environment and your internal state of being. Sometimes just being cognizant of the reason you are experiencing a particular emotion will help you to deal with that emotion. You know it is that "I'm so glad I'm not crazy" realization.

> **Think About It:**
> **What are the things that make you happy?**

Seeking Out the Lord

"For I know the plans I have for you," says the Lord. "they are plans for good and not for disaster, to give you a future and a hope. In those days when you pray I will listen. If you look for me wholeheartedly, you will find me." (Jeremiah 29:11-13 NLT) With God, we have hope. He hears our prayers. He has plans for us. Part of living with intention means intentionally seeking out the Lord. Listening to Him because He is listening to you. Do you know what His plans for you are? Have you heard God tell you that He wants you to do something or to help someone? If you are intentional during your prayer time, God will guide you. Make sure you are making time to listen to Him.

What Is My Intention Anyway?

What is your calling? If you are still waiting for a response, then try out some possibilities. Similar to trying on jeans, it may take a while before you find just the right fit. You can offer to help parents or teachers at the school or be part of the social committee at your church. You can make an inquiry at your local shelter, food bank, or bloodmobile as to ways you can be of service. I understand that social service work may not be for everyone but spreading the word about the love of Christ should be. As you go through volunteer opportunities, you may find that one sparks an interest for you, providing that fulfillment you are seeking. If nothing sparks an interest that is okay, at least you were out there making some positive contributions to your community. Living with intention means being intentional about fulfilling your God-given calling. This should include being intentional about working on your life goals (check that vision board) as well as devotion to family and friends.

"Rejoice always, pray continually, give thanks in all circumstances; for this is God's will for you in Christ Jesus." (1 Thessalonians 5:16-18 NIV) Pray and show gratitude. Think about when you have given presents to people, be it coworkers, friends or family. How does it make you feel when they tell you they love the gift? How about when you see them later and they are using your gift? It makes you feel appreciated. Can you remember a time when you put thought and effort into obtaining a present for someone, and barely got a thank you? How did that make you feel? Now think about how God feels when we do not show gratitude to Him. He has given us the greatest gift of all, our lives, and our loved ones. We need to show Him our appreciation.

The Task List

The task list, also known as the to-do list is often what people think of when hearing the phrase "Being intentional" and of course, this list is a wonderful place to start. Before reading forward, look at your to-do list. What kinds of things are on it? Work items? Household chores? Please tell me that you do indeed have such a list. For me, this list has often been trivial–putting out trash cans on trash day, changing the litter box, picking up groceries, etc. Everyone has errands to run but this is not what "living the life" is about. Sure, you may be intentional in getting your chores finished but does your list include quality time activities with loved ones? Guess what? If you do not make your bed today it will still be there tomorrow. Don't get me wrong, we need tidy houses, and we function better in clean environments. What I am talking about here goes back to setting your priorities.

Of all the tasks we spend our time on in a day, only a small percentage of those activities are related to our life goals. This follows the Pareto Principle, named after Italian economist Vilfredo Pareto which is "The idea that 20% of the effort, or input leads to 80% of the results or output." Take a look at how you spend your day. Are you spending a great deal of time and energy on low-level tasks? Are there any tasks that can be outsourced? For instance, does your lawn need to be mowed? Of course, it does, and by having the neighborhood boy mow it, you are helping him to work and earn money. By giving him your business, you are freeing up time in order to engage in more life-changing activities toward your own goals.

To determine whether something is truly important ask yourself "Will this matter in five years?" Make sure that your daily activities are investments being made towards your future. For example, when you are studying, you are making an investment to pass a class so that you can earn

Living with Intention: Seizing Opportunities

a degree. We also make investments in the people in our lives, through being there for them. The key here is to ask yourself "Which actions will give me the most return on my investments of time, effort, and resources?" Here is a question to ask yourself several times each day: "What would be the best use of my time right now?" Look at the items on your list. Are you working on your most important tasks? You can free up time by picking up your groceries curbside, but you can't outsource your treadmill time or studying for that exam. A good way to prioritize your activities is to think of the items that only you can do for yourself.

If you are the kind of person who reads this type of book, then you are also the sort of person who keeps a planner. Each month conduct an evaluation to determine what you accomplished. It is too easy to allow the little crises that arise in life to derail you from your intentions. When you review the month do you find yourself making excuses? "Oh, that was the month the basement flooded so I couldn't put aside any extra money towards the family vacation." It's okay if you don't attain all your intentions, just ensure that you are cognizant of the reasons behind it.

Life is meant to be enjoyed. Hopefully, you are going out and living life to the fullest. By this, I don't just mean getting out of the house. When you go out, do you savor your experiences? When you socialize, are you intentional in the way you spend money? Or do you arrive home only to realize that you spent half your grocery allowance on appetizers, drinks, and raffle tickets? Are you making memories and creating bonds with friends and family? There are fifty-two weekends in a year. How are you spending them? Are you putting in extra hours at work? Catching up on housework? Resting? Spending time with the kids? I give no judgment on any of these, as long as this is the manner in which you intend to spend your time. Ask yourself, are you spending your time in this manner because you want to or merely out of laziness? Use discernment when making your choices. Please tell me you are not just scrolling social media in all that free time. If your goals involve building finances, then working on your weekend off is a wise choice. If building relationships is important to you, then socializing is an appropriate choice. Review the past week. Have you made your life better or worse? Have you coasted through the week making no changes or improvements to your situation? Are you closer or farther away from obtaining the goals you set for yourself? Is anyone else's life a little better this week because of you?

Have You Found Your Why?

Are you aware of the reasons for doing the things you do? This is commonly referred to as your "Why?" in life. For example, why do you go to work each day? Is it because you find meaning in your profession, or is it merely to pay the bills? We often spend a great deal of time making inquiries of others, but we must also make a habit of questioning ourselves.

It is easy to fall into a lifestyle out of convenience. As adults, we become exceptionally good at letting life get in the way. We also become adept at making excuses and rationalizing our choices. Be open-minded and question the details of your life. We tend to overcomplicate things in life that should be simple. As we discussed earlier, simple does not equal easy and there is no reason to complicate your situation.

To change one's lifestyle and have it be a success requires purposeful reflection. This relates directly to my own journey. I reached a point in my life where I graduated college and obtained a "good government job". I absolutely hated this dead-end job and felt stressed by the toxic people I worked with. I had a long-term relationship end and the fact that most of my closest friends were getting married did not help my social life. I decided that I did not like where my life was headed, and I certainly did not want to wind up being a spinster. I realized that the best vehicle for change was going back to school to obtain my graduate degree. I investigated my options and because I could not afford to stop working, found that attending a program part-time was the best way for me to obtain that degree. Then it hit me, I could continue to work at my job full-time and go to classes part-time for four years and my life would not have to change. My life would not have to change! Whoa, wait a minute, I knew I was defeating my purpose here. I wanted my life to change and was not willing to wait the four years it would take to obtain my master's degree so that I could move forward in my career. I knew I did not enjoy living in the geographical area I was residing in. I needed to make a real change. So, I found a graduate school in San Antonio, quit my job, and moved halfway across the country to start a life I knew I would enjoy. I was not running from anything; I was orchestrating my future. I felt confident in the decision I made and only had one minute of hesitation. It was the morning of my last day at my job. I remember brushing my teeth, looking into the mirror, and thinking "Wow, there's no going back now". I was moving sixteen hundred miles from home to an area where I did not know a soul. During my last hour on the job, an elderly senior secretary took me aside and spoke to me. "What are you doing?" she asked. "You have got a good secure government job. You could have this job for the rest of your life. Why would you just choose to leave it?" She obviously did not know me. I hated this job with a passion. It was not related to my college degree. It didn't even pay well. The thought of having it for the rest of my life sounded like a lifetime of misery. It just cemented in my mind that I was making the right decision. That was almost thirty years ago, and it was one of the best decisions I have ever made. It was a turning point in my life. I am not saying that if you are feeling a little discontented in your current situation, you should quit your job and move halfway across the country. I am saying that you should evaluate the various areas of your life and take a look at where you are going. Do you know the reason you are headed that way? Do you like the direction in which you are facing?

"No, dear brothers and sisters, I have not achieved it, but I focus on this one thing: Forgetting the past and looking forward to what lies ahead, I press on to reach the end of the race and receive the Heavenly prize for which God, through Christ Jesus, is calling us." (Philippians 3:13-14 NLT) Hopefully, you have made good choices that laid a healthy foundation for your life. Regardless of whether it was positive or negative, your past should not control or define you. We should be looking forward rather than behind. We cannot change the past, but we can change our future. We have a Heavenly prize to look forward to and glorifying God along with sharing our love of Him should be part of that future.

Making a Difference in Someone's Life

To have a positive impact on a person's life, isn't this what life is about? We need to seek ways to add value to the lives of the people we encounter. Of course, we want to be a positive influence on our family and friends, but we should also make a positive impact on coworkers and acquaintances. Your cheerful attitude and willingness to help, although not immediately acknowledged by others, will be remembered and appreciated. Try to make being of service to others a staple of your life. Think about how you want to be remembered.

A Life Plan

In their book, *Living Forward*, Hyatt and Harkavy explain creating a life plan. They discuss how some people just rely on the flow of life to take them places. Before realizing it, one can end up in a place they never thought they would be. I would say that these people end up off course, but it is hard to be off course if you never had a plan in the first place. As with any plan, start with the end in mind and map out ways in which to get there. Think about being invited to an event. You have the address of an unfamiliar location. Would you just get in the car and start driving? No, you would probably get on your phone and bring up directions. You would look at the steps listed to get an idea of how you would get there. You would not want to waste your time and gas just driving around. You would want to get to your destination as quickly as possible. The same is true in life. When we decide that we want something, we usually want it as soon as possible. Having a roadmap to obtain these wants is the quickest way to get there.

Sure, life gets messy, and it can throw you off course which is the reason for frequent review and tweaking of plans. You may even decide, as many people do, that what you originally thought you wanted has changed and that is okay. Oftentimes, as we age, we outgrow certain desires. Make sure if you change your mind about a goal, that it is because you no longer desire that goal as opposed to being discouraged when the work gets difficult and tedious. Remember that when working on goals we must put in that demanding work up front before earning our prize. According to Proverbs 13:4 "…lazy people want much but get little, while the diligent are prospering" (TLB). Don't be afraid of hard work!

When shopping these days, it is common to use a credit card. In this manner, you obtain merchandise immediately and pay the credit card bill later. Sometimes, however, before you have made all your payments on the card, the thrill you had in your item begins to diminish. Usually, this is because it was an impulse purchase. Despite losing its appeal, you continue to be obligated to make these payments.

Several years ago, stores had what was called layaway. After making a small deposit, you could choose merchandise, usually a big-ticket item, and the store would hold it for you.

You would make payments until it was paid off and only then would you receive the merchandise. There would typically be a time limit from the store, usually six months, to complete this transaction. The concept of layaway is similar to working on your goals. You must pay upfront, through the work you put in, and then you reach your goal. When we choose the immediate gratification route, like using a credit card, we get our prize immediately. Either way, the item may lose its appeal. I would rather do that work up front (like layaway) and be able to enjoy my prize after it was earned knowing my work was complete.

Having a life plan is similar to following the driving directions on our phone or making those payments on our layaway. We have a plan to obtain what we want. The road to get there may be rough and we may question ourselves, during this process, as to whether we really want this goal after all. This is the reason we investigate our rationale or "Why?" when clarifying a goal. If we have a clear reason for our chosen goal, then it makes the process of working on it seem worthwhile. When the going gets rough, remind yourself to trust the process.

Distractions

There can be no denying that life, especially these days, consists of a series of distractions. If we are not responding to the beeps and chirps from our phones, then we are checking these phones to ensure we have not missed any messages. Think of how many times you check your phone each day. Yes, it feels good when you get a message, but think about the effects it has on your relationships. Can you be fully present when you gather with family for dinner? I will admit that when meeting up with friends, having a cell phone to spend time on is a great relief from the awkwardness of being alone while waiting for them. Unfortunately, it also provides a buffer to limit interaction with other people.

When it comes to seeking intentionality in life, cell phones, and social media use are the first issues I think of. The mobile devices which were intended to allow us the freedom to leave our homes and offices without missing a call are the very minions that take time away from our loved ones. Technology is addictive so we must focus on the advantages it can provide us. Texting has allowed me to respond in a civil manner when I receive an unusual request. I now take pictures all the time and have family members on video. Social media has allowed me to reconnect with people I would have otherwise lost touch with. A cell phone is not a bad thing, but it must be used wisely. Make sure that when you are with family and friends you are fully present with them. Look people in the eyes during conversations. Check your phone later. Your cell phone can easily be replaced, unlike friends and family who are precious.

Seize Your Opportunities

In his book, *Intentional Living*, John Maxwell talks about the importance of living with urgency and seizing opportunities. He states, "If you're going to have a bias in a direction, have a bias toward action. In the end, people most often regret the chances they failed to take, not the chances they took that failed. "Don't just talk about doing something, act on it. The longer you put something off the more likely it is that you will not follow through. Life will naturally present us with some opportunities. Most of the "good" opportunities in life, however, are the ones we create ourselves. I believe that we can create possibilities through the chain reaction of those opportunities with which we seize. This is similar to your social calendar: the more social events you attend, the more you will be invited to. If you constantly decline social events, people will stop inviting you. Make deliberate choices in life rather than merely accepting things as they are. In the example I discussed about my choosing to uproot my life and move to Texas, no one presented me with an opportunity to move or go to graduate school. I just looked at my life and decided that it was pointed in a direction that I did not wish to go so I changed it. Changing your direction might not be so dramatic.

There are numerous ways to change the trajectory of your life. For instance, the more we help others, the more we are sought out by others for assistance. Acknowledge these requests of help from others as God's way of showing you His plan for your life. Keep your eyes open for ways in which to provide aid. Helping others can be life-changing and provide us with opportunities for personal growth. As I stated in our vision board chapter, when you put your intentions in the front of your mind, options will begin to present themselves. More than likely, these opportunities were always there, only you failed to recognize them. Once we have clarity in what we are seeking, we will then recognize these opportunities.

So far in this book, we have explored identifying the stage of life you are in and what you want out of life as well as learning to set goals. Hopefully, you are working from a big-picture view of your life to decide where you want to go. Choices in terms of finances and time management should be consciously made with long-term goals in mind. Some of these long-term goals can be broken down into a series of manageable stepping stones that can be considered as your short-term goals. Being intentional about how you are living your life and the choices you make will ensure that you do not wind up on the wrong track. It will also ensure that you are cherishing the different phases of your life as you go through the process of attaining your goals.

Your Turn:

At the end of the month take a look at your planner. Make a list of the social engagements you attended:

_____

_____

_____

Make a list of social invites you declined as well as the reason you declined:

_____

_____

_____

Beside each item on both lists, put a "Yes" or "No" as to whether or not you are pleased with the decision you made.

"Do not wait: The time will never be 'just right'."
- Napoleon Hill

Chapter 9

The Comfort Zone: Practicing Emotional Yoga

The comfort zone, we have all heard of it. It has become a commonly used phrase. The perception of the safety associated with our comfort zone makes it seem appealing. If someone told you they thought you were living your life in your comfort zone, how would you feel about it? Would you consider it an insult or a compliment? In order to keep growing as a person you must break out of your comfort zone, but there are also times it can be appropriate to bask in it.

What is the Comfort Zone?

What is this comfort zone and why do we keep hearing about it? Just the word "comfort" makes me feel cozy with thoughts of being curled up on a couch in my pj's sipping hot cocoa—or is it just me? When we talk about the comfort zone, however, words such as "stagnant", "predictable", and "rut" are discussed. A comfort zone is a state of being in which you feel comfortable and relaxed with where you are at a particular point in life. It evokes a feeling of being in control. Sometimes, it can refer to a specific compartment of your life. You may be feeling comfortable in your career, your relationship, or with your workout routine. I think we keep hearing about the comfort zone because it serves others. Employers want their employees to grow and stretch themselves; in doing so, they can increase productivity. Health gurus will tell you to get out of your comfort zone so you can become more fit. Whether it is losing weight, increasing those weightlifting reps, or decreasing your A1C, we all have something we can improve upon in this area. While we are in this process of self-improvement, we can become good consumers: by paying for weight loss programs, gym memberships, and personal trainers. Even though it may seem like a marketing ploy, it is still important to evaluate your life, and determine if you have fallen victim to the "comfort zone". Everyone wants a life of comfort, but somehow, over time, that comfort can become a noose.

Is the Comfort Zone Always a Bad Thing?

Comfort can serve us. Who wants to go through life stressed out? I want to enjoy life; I don't want to give myself an ulcer. Life should not be a series of struggles. You need to have time to slow down and appreciate where you are. It is okay to feel comfortable in life, there will be seasons when you need to stay in your comfort zone.

When my husband was diagnosed with stage 3 colon cancer, I went into crisis intervention mode. My primary focus was keeping him alive. I put my career on hold. I knew I had to work, but needed to coast so I could put all my energy into my husband's healthcare. Between his medical treatments and trying to spend quality time together, my husband was all I wanted to concentrate on. I have never regretted that choice. I had my priorities in order. I knew my time with him was limited and I felt anxious. This was not a time to purposefully leave my comfort zone. Putting a hold on my career as well as other big life changes, I was aware that I was in crisis mode. What I did not know, however, was that I really was getting out of my comfort zone—just not by choice. This was one of life's events that forced me out of my zone, only I did not realize it until after the fact.

When you evaluate your life to decide whether it is time to leave your comfort zone, check to see if you might already be out there. If you are in a period of crisis, you will need the comfort and familiarity of your normal routine to get through it. If, upon reflection, you find this not to be a time of crisis, you might want to determine if you are enjoying the comfort zone too much. This often happens when we are recuperating from a season of crisis. We become so accustomed to being in crisis intervention mode in one area that we neglect other areas of our lives. For instance, are you still feeling the effects of COVID restrictions, or have you moved on?

Fear

I often hear people talk about fears they experience such as fear of heights, spiders, public speaking, and death to name a few. Most of these fears are rooted in a deeper meaning such as an apprehension of losing control, public ridicule, being alone, as well as dealing with the unknown. All scary stuff. So why would you purposely expose yourself to these? We expose ourselves to these fears because we need some tension in order to grow. In his book, *Why Courage Matters*, John McCain states, "Fear is the opportunity for courage..." Notice he didn't state that fear was unacceptable or weak. Feeling fear is a normal human response to a stressor, to what we interpret as a threat either physical or emotional. Our response to that fear, however, can be life-defining. Fear is not necessarily a bad thing; it keeps us alert and safe. When we acknowledge the feeling of fear we can exhibit several responses. Acting with courage is one of those responses. It is a common belief that courage is acting despite the fear one may be exhibiting. Fear is the element that makes courage so admirable.

Perhaps you have heard the terms fight or flight. Physiologist Walter Bradford Cannon is given the credit for coining those terms back in the year 1915. In very general terms, this refers to the fact that when given what we perceive as a threat, we may either confront it head-on (fight) or run from it in an effort to avoid the situation (flight). Notice that the important factor here is what we *perceive* to be a threat. What you perceive to be a threat may differ from what others perceive as a threat. Upon further research, I have discovered that the terms freeze and fawn have now been added regarding the study of acute response to stress. For the purpose of my discussion, I will just refer to fight, flight, and freeze. I like to acknowledge this third option of freezing because not everyone will respond to a stressor. Some people fight, some flee, while others will just freeze, thus failing to respond to a threat. This may be due to processing delays such as shock or merely not knowing how they should respond. (Remember our discussion of not making a decision being a decision.) If you choose to respond to a perceived threat, make sure it is a conscious choice. Recognize the feeling of fear and acknowledge your initial response to it. Are you ready to fight? Are you running from the situation? Are you trying to people-please yourself out of the predicament? Are you frozen by indecision?

We all experience fear. We need to ensure that we can conquer our fears and anxieties and not allow them to control us. According to Joyce Meyer, in her book, *Do It Afraid* "If you are allowing fear to rule your decisions, you are missing the good life God has planned for you". You do not want to miss out on any of the good things in life. Face your fears so you can move forward toward these good things life has to offer.

> We can conquer our fears and anxieties and not allow them to control us.

Will it Really be that Bad?

When trying to push out of your comfort zone, you may discover that you are in a battle against yourself. You want to engage in certain social activities but have a sense of trepidation. Some of your fears may be justified but often may be blown out of proportion. There is a type of cognitive behavioral therapy created by the psychotherapist Albert Ellis called Rational Emotive Behavior Therapy (REBT). According to REBT, "The best way to cope with any problem, physical or emotional, was to stop 'catastrophizing' and to do something to correct it." Viewing challenges as possible catastrophes throws us into crisis mode. These anxieties are often due to what REBT refers to as "Irrational beliefs." Basically, we end up working ourselves into a frenzy. You may want to ask yourself: "Would it really be that bad if I were rejected in a particular situation?" "Would my world really come crashing down?" "Would I really die of embarrassment?" Of course, we should look at the risk involved in any given situation. Thinking about the worst possible outcome can help us to prepare both physically and emotionally in case this were to actually happen. Most of these worst-case scenarios, however, rarely occur, thus resulting in needless worry. I have always been of the notion, to hope for the best and plan for the worst.

Imagine a life where you don't take risks. Life would be easy. Pain would be minimal, yet there will still be pain, whether we take those calculated risks or not. In terms of breaking out of your comfort zone, Ellis advises you to "Practice making yourself as uncomfortable as you can be, in order to eradicate your irrational fears and become unanxious and comfortable later". This desensitization to a stressful stimulus is referred to in psychology as habituation.

It works well when you have time to think about the issue that is making you feel uncomfortable.

Think about the people you know who get stressed out by any little thing. Now think about those people who are totally chill. Which one would you rather be? We can talk ourselves into anxiety. We have also learned that we can challenge our fears and talk ourselves out of anxiety. If you are particularly anxious or stressed, you may want to conduct a body scan. A body scan is often used in the practice of yoga during the final phase of the class called Savasana. Focus on your body, tensing and releasing your muscles starting out with the toes, and slowly work your way up the entire body. Take notice of where the tensions are in your body. Acknowledge those tensions you are responding to from the outside environment. This process can relax both the mind and the body. According to international yoga teacher Noah Mazé, "Savasana stimulates the parasympathetic nervous system (your rest and digest response) and calms your sympathetic nervous system (your fight, flight and freeze response). You will be deeply chilled out after Savasana, and everyone around you will appreciate you even more."

Introverts and Extroverts

When discussing the comfort zone, I cannot help but think about the two main personality types and how they respond to life events. The two main personality types I am referring to are introverts and extroverts. The concept of these terms was proposed by the Swiss Psychiatrist and Psychoanalyst Carl Jung. Of course, we all know that introverts are the shy ones and extroverts are the outgoing ones but there is more to this simplistic assessment. A person can not be judged by what is seen portrayed on the outside. Introversion and extroversion are traits on a continuum. There will be people who are on the extreme end with most falling somewhere in the middle, leaning to one of the sides. It is not uncommon to see what appears to be an outgoing introvert. When an introvert finds themselves in a familiar and comfortable environment, such as their daily work site, they may appear very outgoing. If you do not know the person, you may misinterpret them as being an extrovert. The main difference between introverts and extroverts is where they absorb their energy. Each person may find themselves mingling at a party, and both appear to be outgoing. Later that evening, at home, the extrovert feels energized, while the introvert feels the need to plug back in and recharge their emotional battery.

According to the book *The Essential Jung*, Anthony Storr reports that when referring to introverts "...relations with other people become warm only when safety is guaranteed, and when he can lay aside his defensive distrust. All too often he cannot, and consequently, the number of friends and acquaintances is very restricted". This refers to that small circle of close friends to which introverts often cling to. Storr continues on to state that extroverts have "A desire to influence and be influenced by events, a need to join in...", he continues on to report that the extrovert "...lives in and through others". This is the social butterfly we all know and love. So, when it comes to getting out of the comfort zone, what being out of the zone for an introvert looks like is very different compared to what an extrovert considers out of their zone. One size does not fit all. You may find introverts taking more emotional risks while extroverts take more social risks, it just depends on the person's level of ease threshold. You do not need to compare your attempts with getting out of your comfort zone to anyone else's attempts. This is not a competition; it is your attempt at living your own best life. You are not trying to impress anyone—unless, of course, it is yourself!

Happiness and the Comfort Zone?

I am reminded of an episode of Friends, where Monica gets a date from a guy whom she had a crush on in high school; his name was Chip. She asks him where he works, and he tells her "You know where I work". Apparently, in his late twenties, he never left his first job. "Like I'd give up that job! Free popcorn and candy any time I want!" Longevity with an employer is not a bad thing, as a matter of fact, I admire it. It shows persistence and dedication. However, unless it is your own business, there is no need for that level of dedication. If you are at a job for any length of time you should be moving up in the company. I am not saying to up and quit your job, just ensure that if you maintain your current position, you are growing and learning in your field.

Now back to the scenario with Monica and Chip. When she asks him if he still lives at home with his parents he says "Yes", and she is done with him. Why? She felt he was going nowhere in life, but here is the clincher—it was not her determination to make. If you look at the clip, you will see that Chip seems quite happy. Isn't happiness our goal? Yes! Eventually, however, happiness fades. The timespan on this will vary from person to person. Happiness can slowly creep away until you find yourself evaluating life and asking how you let the years slip by without making any changes. Most people acknowledge that while they enjoy having fun, they realize that these times cannot last forever. There are goals that need to be attained. No matter how much fun you are having, eventually, there is a time to get back to work.

My idea of living a life to the fullest means being happy and praising the Lord while living out his will for my life. Sometimes, discovering what God's will is for your life can be confusing. We should focus on the things that we know make God happy. We know it pleases Him when we do our best at tasks, however menial they may be. Reading the Word, praising Him, and of course, introducing others to Him are things that we can focus on in our search for His will in our lives.

> Living a life to the fullest means being happy and praising the Lord while living out his will.

Think About It:
Are you living your life according to a plan or by default?

Routines and the Comfort Zone

Sometimes it can be difficult to determine if you are in your comfort zone. In order to accomplish the tasks of daily living and working toward our goals, we need to establish routines. These routines help us to function: doing laundry, grocery shopping, meal prepping, housecleaning, exercising, etc. We can get so accustomed to our routines that it becomes our default setting. How do you feel about your daily routine? If you eat the same thing for lunch every day, can you tell me your reason for doing this? Do you enjoy it? Does it serve a purpose? Is there a reason you eat yogurt at lunch every day? Is it to get in your calcium, because it is inexpensive, or just easy to throw in a lunchbox? Are you living life according to a plan or on default mode? Being cognizant of the choices you are making in your life is important. When and how to break out of your comfort zone is based on your personality type as well as your current stage of life.

For many years I have driven the same model car. I drove my last car for over twenty-one years. It had a weird setup under the stereo for cup holders. It only allowed for a twelve-ounce cup and there really wasn't an option to hold anything larger. So, each day I took a twelve-ounce cup of coffee to work. Finally, I got a new car and continued to take my twelve-ounce cup of coffee to work with me. One day, it hit me: "My cup holders are very large in this new vehicle! Why am I taking such a small container of coffee with me?" I felt silly when I realized that, for a month, I was taking my little twelve-ounce coffee with me out of default! Today, in that same car, I now happily bring my sixteen-ounce tumbler of coffee with me. We all get into habits. Make sure your rationale for these habits is up to date.

Sometimes life forces us out of our comfort zone; "Congratulations, you're pregnant!", "We're sorry, but we are experiencing a reduction in workforce." Sometimes just the pure movement of life will thrust us forward, such as graduating from school, but now what do you do? Unfortunately, this is how many people move along through the phases of their lives, not purposefully making an effort to change but allowing life to move them along as if they are waves in the ocean. Some of these people fall backward into success. For instance, I had a friend who defaulted on her student loans. As a consequence, she had her wages garnished, not something anyone would purposefully choose. As a result of this, she paid off her student loans whereas I continued, like a turtle, slowly paying my loans. I must say, I was a little jealous. Sure, these unplanned events can move a person forward in life but there are many times when life does not send us such opportunities. We must create our own future. This may seem like a daunting task. Many times, we wait, stating that we don't feel ready. The fact is, in life, most of the time we will not feel ready, but we must proceed anyway. If not now, when? What are you waiting for?

"Yes, come, Jesus said. So Peter went over the side of the boat and walked on the water toward Jesus." (Matthew 14:29 NLT) Because he felt supported, Peter walked on water but then he doubted, and he faltered. This shows me we can do insurmountable things when we feel confident. Confidence is power. It also reminds me that walking toward Jesus is always a good choice.

As Soon as...

"As soon as I lose weight, I'll have my photo taken, ...wear a bathing suit, ...run that marathon." Sure, we want to be prepared before taking action but the whole "As soon as..." thought process can be dangerous thinking. Ask any elderly person, and they will laugh as they reflect upon their younger years. They also thought they looked bad, and now that they are old, they wished they could look that good. Remember how you felt about your own looks twenty years ago? Yes, it would be ideal if you could take that family photo when you looked your best, but (and not to sound negative) what if it goes the other way and you look worse? What if that special family member passes away? I'm not saying you shouldn't strive to be your best but at a certain point, you must set a follow-through deadline. (Yes, I said deadline not target date!) Do it anyway—do it with some errors, do it tired, do it fat! When we think of regrets, we usually think of those things we failed to do and the chances we did not take. Sure, there will be times when we wish we had prepared ourselves better, but if we wait for the perfect circumstances we could be waiting forever. Maybe you don't feel quite ready for that marathon. Do it anyway, and you know what? You can also have a re-do later. Just get out there!

Why Didn't I Do That?

Many authors and social media influencers will say to try something new each day in order to get out of your comfort zone. Personally, I don't want to. After all, do I really need to get so far out that I lose the essence of me? The aim of getting out of your comfort zone should not be to lose yourself, it should be to enhance yourself so that you are the best possible version of you. Have you ever asked, "Why didn't I do that"? Maybe it was getting up on stage at a karaoke bar where you saw a person having a good time singing. Perhaps it's getting out on the dance floor alone or with a partner. When you are out and about, I am sure that you are people-watching. It's hard not to watch people and observe others having fun. How about when watching television or videos, do you see the appearance of happy people? You should. Marketing and advertising companies spend a great deal of money, making people appear happy using their products in order to boost sales. Even knowing that these people are being paid to appear happy, it is still enticing.

I recently went ziplining. The thought of being suspended in the air by merely a cable was a little scary to me. Now, I am not a thrill seeker just for the heck of it, but I do love a good aerial view, so I decided to go for it. As I waited my turn to be hooked in, there were waivers to sign. If that does not instill fear in you, I don't know what would! As everyone signed the waivers, there were many jokes heard ranging from whether people had their wills up to date to figuring a graceful way out of the line. Many times, people make jokes when they are nervous. As I stood on the platform awaiting my turn, I felt scared. I questioned myself as to why I was doing this, "Why would I pay good money to feel this huge knot in my stomach"? Then it was time. "Yikes!" ...and then "...wait a minute ...aww, pretty"—what a wonderful experience it was. It was so beautiful! When it was over, I was glad

I had pushed through the fear and did it! Then, of course, I promptly posted about it on social media.

Our social media accounts are online memory books, digitally keeping track of our life experiences. Some people feel the need to post frequently. Whether you post frequently or not, you know if you are proud of the experiences you are allowing in your life. Maybe you scroll through social media pondering if you will ever have the type of excitement that you see in that post of a "friend of a friend". You wonder what it would be like to post an adventurous pic of your own. Maybe sitting out during karaoke or declining that person's dance request is not life-changing—or is it?

Small Things Add Up

It's the small moments in life that add up to become big memories. Small changes can yield large results. The small dietary decisions that cause us to either gain or lose weight. The small financial decisions that lead us to either a healthy savings account or a frightening credit card statement. We need to keep track of these small activities, but we shouldn't stress over them. If we splurge and have a piece of birthday cake at the office, we will not immediately become 500 pounds. However, if this becomes the norm, then it can become a problem. Making small changes to our daily lives is a great way to build confidence. With each healthy choice made, there is a mental check mark that enables you to feel good in having made that positive step forward. Showing courage involves an act of bravery—it means being scared and doing it anyway. Are you performing small acts of bravery?

Ideas for Getting Out of Your Comfort Zone

In this section, I am going to discuss a few ideas for getting out of your comfort zone. These range from social risks such as telling someone how you feel about them, and reaching out to old friends to genre risks such as trying out new music and movie choices. Maybe getting out of your comfort zone involves accepting a social invitation that you would normally decline or dining alone. These are small areas where you can practice emotional stretching. I placed them into categories that apply to myself, but I hope it will give you some ideas that you can apply to your own situation. I've also included a Comfort Zone Escape Bingo card if you would like to make a game out of it.

Hopefully, this list will spark personal ways in which you can take a risk in your own life. I made my list in categories according to levels of engagement (beginner, intermediate, and advanced), so that you can choose based on how far out of your comfort zone you would like to go. Notice that these tasks also tend to be separated into risk categories. Physical (may involve risk of physical harm to oneself) such as going mountain climbing. Emotional (may involve risk of being rejected) such as telling someone how you feel about them. Financial (may involve losing money) such as making an investment with no return.

Beginner – Eat at a new restaurant, change your driving route, give someone a compliment, try a new beauty treatment, listen to a new style of music, watch a movie or television genre untypical for you, cook a new recipe, invite someone to church, attend church service at a different time, or engage in a new form of exercise.

Intermediate – Wear a new hairstyle, try a new hair color, participate in an escape room, accept a social invitation you normally would decline, go out in public in an outfit that differs from your usual style, see your doctor about that concern you have, declutter, attend the funeral service, call a potential client, apply for the promotion, drive in bad weather, volunteer when you hear someone ask for help, or join a committee. Take an item from the beginner list and bring it to the next level. For example, in the beginner list you cooked a new recipe, now try taking that dish to your next church social.

Advanced – Go to a social event alone, complete a bucket list item, contact an old friend you haven't spoken to in ages, sing karaoke, visit a new church, strike up a conversation with a stranger, go on a date with the person you met online, donate blood, take a dance lesson, tell someone how you feel about them, start a DIY project, travel to a new destination, or check out a sensory deprivation tank. Take an item from the intermediate list and bring it to the next level. For example, in the intermediate list you volunteered when you heard someone ask for help, now become the leader of a volunteer project.

Comfort Zone Escape Bingo

Try a new hairstyle	Complete a bucket list item	Sing karaoke	Donate blood for a good cause	Travel to a new place
Listen to unfamiliar music	Try a new beauty treatment	Prepare a new recipe	Take a dance lesson	Declutter a room in your house
Try a new restaurant	Give someone a compliment	Visit a new church	Change your driving route	Volunteer
Go to an escape room	Accept a social invitation	Say hello to a stranger	Wear a different outfit	Invite someone to church
Go it alone	Contact an old friend	Try a new form of exercise	Do a DIY project	Try some sensory deprivation

Risk Taking

"Be strong! Be courageous! Do not be afraid of them! For the Lord your God will be with you. He will neither fail you nor forsake you." (Deuteronomy 31:6 TLB) This tells me that God's got your back! It acknowledges that we may be afraid but reminds us that we don't have to be. There are no guarantees in life. We will, during several times in our lives, have to take risks whether we want to or not. Then there will be those times we choose to take some risks in order to forge a better life. Hopefully, during those times, you will engage in educated risk-taking while relying on the Lord for guidance. Any risk, however, even a highly planned-out one, may result in a loss. There is no guarantee of success every time. If you do find yourself on the losing end of a risk, be sure to learn the lesson from that experience. Don't stop working toward your goals just because something did not work out the way you planned. Sometimes our failures turn out to be blessings in disguise.

There is no need to feel timid when we know we have the power of the Lord within us. "For the Spirit God gave us does not make us timid, but gives us power, love, and self-discipline." (2 Timothy 1:7 NIV) I love the fact that self-discipline is acknowledged in this scripture. With the inner power God gives us we are able to summon self-discipline. With the Lord, we can do anything!

In this chapter, we learned that the comfort zone refers to the way we live our lives in a manner that is comfortable and routine for us. We will live our lives on autopilot if we are not careful. Being in the comfort zone is not necessarily a bad thing. It is enjoyable to have a relaxing life. In times of crisis, being in the comfort zone can provide us with a sense of stability. To grow, however, we will need to step outside of this zone of relaxation. Often when we do this, we experience personal growth and excitement despite the initial feelings of discomfort. Life is like the ocean with a series of ebbs and flows. Enjoy your time in the comfort zone, then go outside of it for a while, it will always be there awaiting your return.

Your Turn:

Review the last three months. List five things you have done outside of your comfort zone. Put a star next to the ones that worked well.

1._____

_____

2._____

_____

3._____

_____

4._____

_____

5._____

_____

Look at the upcoming month. What can you do to get out of your comfort zone?

1. _____

2. _____

3. _____

Section IV

Glorifying the Lord

If you have read this far, then I must say "Congratulations"! Most people do not finish the books they start. Of course, if you are reading this book then you are not like most people. By this point, you have established what you want out of life and have come to the realization that as we go through life our dreams and goals will change depending on the stage of life we are in. Hopefully, you have created your vision board and have written out your goals using the SMART method. You should be living your life in a more intentional manner than before you picked up this book as well as starting to face your fears, so you do not become complacent.

In Sectional IV, we focus on creating meaning for our lives. We will discuss the importance of our relationships and how to be a blessing to others. We cover how to live our lives so that we are glorifying the Lord by living within his will. We acknowledge being grateful for our current stage of life. Although we have dreams and goals, in order to enjoy our lives, we also need to think about our legacy. Living your best life isn't only about yourself, it is about community.

Almighty God,

I want to thank You for allowing me the opportunity to make changes in my life. Thank You for the people You have placed in my path. Thank You for the challenges that have made me grow. Thank You for the mercy and grace You have shown me. Help me to lead a life of glory to You. Help me to seek thoughts and behaviors that are in alignment with Your will. Thank You for my life and all the work You are doing in the background for my future.

Amen

"You know it's love when all you want is that person to be happy, even if you're not part of their happiness."

-Julia Roberts

Chapter 10

Embracing Relationships: Blessing Others

This book is about living your best life. When asking people their ideas about "living the life", the top comments are focused on loved ones: spouse, children, family, and friends. We were created to go through life with the companionship of others. Think of your priorities. Most people would say that their family is their priority, and many would say that family is everything. As complicated and stressful as relationships can be, what would life look like without them? We are not hermits. Making a difference in the lives of others—this is what life is about. We don't get through this world alone. The people in our lives provide us with meaning, and we provide meaning for them. Just as Hillary Clinton said, "It takes a village".

Why Do We Need Relationships?

Relationships offer us community, also known as a sense of belonging. Relationships can also offer us validation. Validation has often received a bad rap. We are told that if we are emotionally healthy, we should not seek validation from others. If you are over the age of eighteen, you should be able to make decisions without requiring input from others. It's okay to seek advice once in a while, just don't allow yourself to become dependent on it. There are many things we can, and should, do independently. However, we will, at times, require some feedback and resources that others can provide. Never believe someone who says they are a self-made man. Receiving validation and advice regarding our life choices and sense of self can be reassuring. There are many times the insight given from a friend can be a game changer in our life. It is a great feeling to have a friend who provides emotional support. Friendship is important and it is acknowledged in Scripture. "Two people are better off than one for they can help each other succeed. If one person falls, the other can reach out and help. But someone who falls alone is in real trouble." (Ecclesiastes 4:9-10 NLT)

We don't get through this world alone and we shouldn't have to try to. Go to your social media memories. Whatever sticks out the most should be the experiences and conversations with people. Look at the pictures on your phone. There are pics of food, nature, and maybe copies of items needed for business, but the truly important ones, the ones that make you smile are the pics of people. In your home do you display pictures? Do you print out the pics from your

Embracing Relationships:Blessing Others

phone or take it a step further by electronically sending pics to friends to make them smile? Embrace your relationships, they are what makes life so very interesting, they are what gives your life meaning.

Who are your Relationships?

There are different categories of relationships: friends, significant others, mentors, family, coworkers, friendlings, and acquaintances. Each category serves a purpose in our lives.

Friends – Their purpose is to provide companionship and support. It is commonly stated that you can tell where someone is going in life by looking at their friends. To put it another way, our friends can either make us or break us. The more time you spend with someone, the more likely you will be receptive to their ways. Maybe you have a friend who has a habit which you do not like. The longer you are friends and spend increased time with them, the more tolerant you become to that behavior whether you admit to it or not.

How do your friends treat you? Keep in mind that we teach others how to treat us by what we tolerate. Do you have a friend you frequently cancel on when you don't feel like going somewhere? "Oh, they won't mind," you think. Then there is that friend you better not cancel on because you just know that if you do, then you won't be invited to go out with them for quite some time. These

> We teach others how to treat us by what we tolerate.

friends have taught you how to treat them. How are you teaching your friends to treat you? What criteria do you have for your friendships?

As far as friends influencing your behavior, try this exercise: List the top five people involved in your life. Next to each person named, list what it is that you like about them. Then give a (+) if they can pull you up or a (-) if they will drag you down.

People	Quality you like	(+) or (-)
#1		
#2		
#3		
#4		
#5		

Are you someone with a wide array of friends or do you have a small intimate circle? Over time, friendships will change. People will come and go out of your life. Some friendships will deepen while others drift away. Not all friendships were made to last a lifetime, many are just for a season. Yes, some seasons will be longer than others.

Modern technology has had an impact on our friendships. There are people who only keep in touch electronically. Is that enough for you? Is your preferred method of communication phone or text? It can often depend on the situation. If it is easier to express things through text, you need to ask yourself why this is so. Are you using modern technology as a shield of protection? In this age of artificial intelligence, our opportunities to encounter real people are diminishing. Even when we have interactions with friends it may be electronically. I have to say thank you for the video chats, if we are communicating electronically at least we can see each other. Regardless of your friendship, learn to enjoy the time you do spend with your friends.

Significant Others – Their purpose is to make you feel loved and desired as well as to provide companionship. Your spouse, fiancé, boyfriend/girlfriend, guy/gal you are dating, that special person you're really attracted to, the "it's complicated" person, however, you chose to label this individual, they are known as your significant other; maybe you have one and maybe you don't. Maybe you are asking God to send you one right now. Regardless of your current situation, I'm sure you have known, at some point in time, what it is like to have a significant other. The purpose of our significant other may change as our life situation changes. These are the relationships that often seem to be complicated; the ones we tend to analyze the most.

Many people have started romances with a partner they have never met in real life. Nowadays, you can literally sit in your living room and meet people online. Social media can help us to start relationships, but it has altered how we end them as well. The advent of various social media platforms has really impacted our relationships. It has often been said that with social media you never have to let go of your friends, there is no goodbye. There are many advantages, unfortunately, there are also disadvantages to this. One disadvantage and it is a big one—do you really want to see how your ex is doing after you have broken up? Of course, you do not know if their posts are sincere, or just a means to show off how well they are doing. Then there are the people who have so many things going on in their lives and they choose not to share anything online. Although you may think you are keeping in touch with them, you only view what they are choosing the public to see. Being able to compare ourselves with others is a double-edged sword. It can help us gauge whether we are on track within our life stage milestones but as anyone with a social media account can attest, sometimes we compare our everyday life to the highlight reel of someone else. This can cause us to create unrealistic expectations, resulting in possible dissatisfaction with a life that should by many accounts, feel blessed. The easiest way to make yourself unhappy is to compare yourself to others.

Mentors – Their purpose is to provide guidance. Since we have covered being influenced by friends, I cannot ignore the importance of the intentional influence through mentors. A mentor is a person who you admire for certain aspects of their life and personality. These mentors can often be found in the workplace as the supervisor who takes the rookie under their wing. Perhaps your mentor is the woman with three children who teaches you the ropes of childrearing. Maybe you have an aspiration but cannot find anyone to emulate. Many times, we turn to the entertainment industry to provide us with a role model. Obviously, these people may not be the best choices. With a mentor, you do not have to aspire to be a carbon copy of the person. We should not worship them! God is the only one we should worship. Because no one is perfect, you may find yourself admiring their business skills, but not the way they handle personal relationships. Focus on the part you want to mirror in your life. If you do not have a personal mentor to guide you, then you can seek guidance through books and online videos.

Family – Their purpose is to provide unconditional love and support. There are different types of families. First, there is your family of orientation which is the family you are born into. This family consists of your parents, siblings, grandparents, aunts, uncles, cousins, etc. Next is your family of procreation, this is the family you have created, your spouse and children. Closeness with family members can be complicated. Oftentimes it is because we have no filters with family. Statements claimed to be said with love can be hurtful. With family, however, they have known you for a lifetime. They know the good, bad, and ugly you have gone through. Negotiating relationships with family is important because these are the people you will be with throughout your life. As friends come and go, family is always there.

Co-workers – Their purpose is to provide a sense of belonging and fulfillment, a sense of purpose. These are people you do not necessarily choose to be around, but due to needing a paycheck, you are thrown into the daily grind together. Close friendships are often formed in the workplace due to shared experiences. These people can range from the boss to peers, subordinates, and customers. The personalities of these people can either help you endure a bad job or cause you to despise your dream job. This is where you need to be careful in determining how much personal information to reveal. Coworkers may appear to be friends when they are merely being friendly. Use discretion when determining which people you work with are friends and which are merely fellow employees who are friendly.

Friendlings – Their purpose is to provide us with a means to practice social skills. These are your fake friends, people you choose to play nice with so as to not cause unnecessary strife in your life. It may be a friend of one of your friends or perhaps an old classmate with whom you no longer have a connection to, it may be a loved one's significant other, or that sweet woman from church who for some reason just always seems to rub you the wrong way. These are often the people you, for some unknown reason, choose to impress, even though they are not your friends. Why do we care to impress people who are not important in our lives? When I think of friendlings I think about that old saying to keep your friends close and your enemies closer.

Acquaintances – Their purpose is fulfilling human interaction and providing varying points of view. These are people we see at the store whose faces we recognize yet have never spoken to. They are also the people we converse with at the airport, knowing we will never see them again. Anyone who has ever used an ATM or pumped gas without having to go into the convenience store knows there is a difference between simply obtaining a service and interacting with a human. When you make phone calls, which do you prefer, talking to a person or the automated system? You may find that without human interaction business is completed rapidly yet you feel a sense that something is missing. Treat everyone you encounter with respect, whether you feel they deserve it or not. It is not your job to judge others. You do not know their history or what they are going through. Perhaps as you begin to display genuine interest in an acquaintance you may make a new friend or confidant.

Shut That Door

Not sure how you feel about someone? For me, the best way to gauge how I feel about someone is my "shut the door", or in some cases "hang up the phone" test. After having an interaction with a person, perhaps a visit or outing, at the end of the evening when I shut my front door I would have a feeling. It ranged anywhere from "He's so sweet", "I can't wait to do this again" to "Idiot!" or "Whew, I'm so glad that's over!" The same applied to phone conversations. I would either feel relieved at ending the conversation or giddy. I had a friend who had the worst time adapting to her new cell phone. Perhaps you have had the experience of finishing a conversation and then had trouble using the end call button on your phone. Well, unfortunately, my friend would do this when talking with her husband. She would think the conversation was over, then immediately state something such as "He is so stupid!" Needless to say, this did not go over well with him. Regardless of what she thought of their phone interaction, she should have kept her mouth shut, at least for a few minutes after the call. This just goes to show we need to make note of our immediate feelings once our time with a person is over.

Relationships and Timing

Relationships may be the reason we delay working on our goals. When taking care of an elderly parent or sick loved one, we need to review our priorities. People are more important than tasks. Waiting until the children are older and more independent is a common reason for creating delays. I remember speaking with a Peace Corps recruiter, many years ago, who told me the number one reason people backed out of the two-year commitment was due to relationships. Some people put off working toward their goals and use family members as the reason. If you fall into this category, make sure your decisions are conscious choices to use your time in this manner and not due to laziness. Don't use your loved ones as an excuse. Using your time and energy to take care of others is noble. Do not allow anyone to tell you otherwise. It may be difficult to watch others get ahead in life while you are in a sacrificial season but having your priorities in order is priceless. People are irreplaceable.

Expectations

In most situations, we have expectations attached to our relationships. For the relationships you deem as "trivial", it may be a simple need, such as at work, when you require a coworker to finish their job so you can do yours. In relationships with family members, it may mean providing you with validation or positive feedback regarding your life decisions. You may have expectations that your spouse will back you up at family functions and other social gatherings. There can be expectations we may not even realize we are imposing upon others. Without this communication about our emotional needs, problems will arise. Do you have relationship requirements you place on loved ones? Have you expressed these expectations to them?

Closure

Not all relationships are meant to last your lifetime. Some of our friendships will tend to drift away. There may be some friendships where a large argument ensues which ends everything. Most of the time, however, it happens that our journey through life encounters forks in the road where we part from friends. No arguments, just taking different paths. Our relationships with significant others will end, until of course we find "The One". These relationships will have a definable ending moment. You may be the one initiating the end or the one getting left behind. You may feel the need for closure. Getting closure can help you figuratively wrap up those emotions in a pretty little box so you can put it away and move on with your life. Closure often comes in the form of a conversation, usually tearful. This can be very cathartic. Other times, however, it does not help. You can express everything you feel you need to but continue to feel more is needed.

Similar to journaling, writing a letter can be a healthy way to seek closure. Giving the letter to your significant other is the goal. A letter is good because it gives you the opportunity to look it over and make changes before sending it on. Passing that letter on, however, may not be possible. Closure with your significant other is not always an option. It would be nice but in reality, you may just have to move on without it. Most of the time you will not get the opportunity for the closure you feel you need. That is okay, because closure, much like forgiveness, is more about you than the other person. How can you achieve this on your own? Write the letter and express everything that is on your heart. There is no need to censor it because you are not passing it on. Read it aloud. Remind yourself that in life there will not always be full closure. Even when there is an opportunity for closure, people will state they do not necessarily feel relieved. Accept this, then dedicate yourself to moving forward.

> Closure, much like forgiveness, is more about you than the other person.

It's Not About You

It may be your life, but it is not all about you. "And here is how to measure it—the greatest love is shown when a person lays down his life for his friends. And you are my friends if you obey me." (John 15:13-14 TLB) In every situation we encounter, we need to factor others into the equation. Our lives influence each other. If you are going through a rough time one of the best things you can do is to find someone to help and then provide that help. Pour your love into others. It takes the focus off yourself and your problems. We want to have a positive influence on others. Our purpose in life is to glorify the Lord. When we wake up in the morning, we should think of how we will honor God on this day as well as how we can be a blessing to others. The greatest blessing, of course, is to bring someone to Christ. Let people know of your love and faith in Christ by being a positive Christian role model.

> **Think About It:**
> **Do you have statements and feelings that need to be communicated to someone in your life?**

Emotional Risk Taking

In dealing with the people in our lives, there will be many opportunities for emotional risk-taking. When we look at breaking out of our comfort zone, taking emotional risks is one way to do so. I think I would rather take a bungee jump than endure an emotionally risky conversation with someone. As uncomfortable as it may be, having these difficult conversations can lead a relationship to a deeper level of closeness. Notice I said conversations, not confrontations. An open conversation is often appreciated by many so that both parties can at least agree to disagree. Many times, it is the lack of conversations which end relationships. Are there statements and feelings that need to be communicated to someone in your life? If the answer is yes, then ask yourself why you have not done so. Determine if there is a reason for this or merely an excuse. Perhaps you have a strategic reason. Life is short and even if you feel you have many healthy days ahead of you, there is no guarantee the other person will be so blessed. Be thinking of ways now to initiate that discussion. It does not have to be a formal event. I think one of the most soul-curdling things to hear from someone is "We have to talk". Your life is not a movie where you need to have a serious sit-down conversation. Think of opportunities you can seize to tell this person what is on your heart. If not now, when? I don't intend to sound dramatic, but if you knew that one year from now, this person would no longer be on Earth, would you feel okay with not having that discussion?

Forgiveness

Forgiveness should be a natural practice in your life. It is definitely not the fun part of relationships. Sometimes feelings will get hurt but we get to choose the way we feel and respond. "Make allowance for each other's faults and forgive anyone who offends you. Remember, the Lord forgave you, so you must forgive others." (Ecclesiastes 3:13 NLT) No one is perfect. We need to accept people for who they are. Let the person be themself. We are not perfect so we cannot expect others to be perfect. It is fine to have high expectations, but perfection is impossible.

During the course of a friendship, disagreements may arise and there may be times when the other person does not feel they are in the wrong. Forgiveness is about your emotional well-being. The practice of forgiveness is not based on receiving an apology from the other person.

Forgiveness is beneficial to both you as well as all those whom you encounter because you are not walking around with bitterness in your heart. Sometimes a person may do something that affects a relationship in a way for which there is no coming back. It is an awful feeling when another person has done damage and possibly ruined your relationship. At least if you were the party at fault, you could feel regret and apologize. You could try to make amends. When it is the other person at fault, you must wait for their next move. You will not always have control in a relationship. There are many things that cannot be reversed. All you can do is move forward.

Moving forward should include not holding a grudge. The other person may ask for forgiveness, or then again, they may not. They may feel remorse or maybe feel they have done nothing wrong. Either way, bitterness should not be held in your heart. Only you can judge if you can move forward in the relationship. Sometimes it means that it is a different relationship altogether. Sometimes it means putting a little distance between you and the person. You get to decide who you are in a relationship with as well as how close you want people to be with you.

Boundaries

Boundaries are a tool used in relationships. Sometimes lack of boundaries will cause problems, while other times it is an over-enforcement of boundaries that becomes an issue. Boundaries, no matter how well-intentioned, will not allow you to change a person. We may be able to influence people but that depends on how receptive the person is. God gave us all free will. A person has control over their own thoughts and choices, whether they acknowledge it or not. This works both ways. You cannot control others and others cannot control you. If you feel controlled by another person, ask yourself if this is a situation which you could walk away from or a situation you are tolerating in order to keep the peace. Sometimes relationships involve power struggles. It is possible to maintain your power in a relationship without compromising who you are. We want to grow in our relationships and not lose ourselves. Setting boundaries enables us to experience relationships with intention.

Setting boundaries enables us to experience relationships with intention.

Trust

Trust is the integrity in a relationship. Are you true to your word? Are you honest when you speak? Do you have your loved ones back? Having a sense of trust is the core of a relationship. It is not comfortable to feel as though you must walk on eggshells around someone. Not knowing if someone will explode emotionally or if they will support you in a difficult situation can make it draining to be around that person. When trust is broken in a relationship it takes work to rebuild. Forgiveness will be in order, most of the time on both sides. Actions will be looked to, rather than merely words, in order to rebuild that trust. Time and patience will be required.

In this age of artificial intelligence, opportunities to encounter people in person are diminishing. When we have interactions with friends, it may be electronically. Make sure to clarify any issues of concern so that a misinterpreted text or typo does not destroy a relationship. I must say that I am grateful for the option to video chat. When we communicate via video, we can see facial expressions and hear those intonations in our voice, which really enhances the clarity of our communication.

Showing Appreciation

The aspect of showing appreciation for others is often neglected. It is easy to get caught up in the busyness of life. We become task-oriented and forget we truly do depend on other people to varying degrees. Although you can state that all you need is the Lord, remember, He is the one who brings people into our lives. These people are often brought through our lives to help us both physically and emotionally. People are also brought into our lives so we can help, teach, and inspire them.

In his book, *The 5 Love Languages*, Gary Chapman discusses the various ways in which people feel loved and appreciated. These "love languages" are not exclusively geared to our significant others. People feel appreciated in different ways. Here is my interpretation of the love languages:

1. Words of Appreciation
2. Acts of Service
3. Gifts

4. Quality Time
5. Touch

Think about the people in your life. Are kind words enough to make your loved ones feel appreciated (Words of Appreciation), or would running an errand (Acts of Service) demonstrate it more strongly? A small token (Gift), or hug (Touch), may make one feel special while the same actions hold no meaning to you. Actions speak louder than words. Having your phone placed out of sight and on silent mode while spending mealtime with your child (Quality Time), is not only a great representation of a role model but demonstrates love in a concrete manner, as opposed to merely stating it. Even the fact that you have spent the mental energy to determine someone's love language shows that you appreciate that person. Don't believe me? Listen to any mother the day after Mother's Day. I am sure she will not be shy in telling you of how her family either planned a thoughtful day for her or just phoned it in. Just as you spend time finding the perfect Christmas gift for each individual on your list, so you should take the time to investigate the love language of the people in your life. Do not assume they want to be shown love in the same manner you do. Just as the gift you buy them is different from what you would purchase for yourself, their love language may also differ from yours.

Investments

Make the most of your relationships. I will even go so far as to say, make the most of all exchanges you have with

Embracing Relationships: Blessing Others

people. Enjoy all those interactions, from that chatty lady at the doctor's office to the sweet security officer at the mall. You never know how much that cordial conversation may mean to someone. People don't walk around screaming "I am lonely!" In actuality, most people try to disguise their feelings of isolation for various reasons, such as feelings of embarrassment. Be kind to everyone. Practice those social skills. Think of that person you need to reach out to and set aside a time to do so.

Relationships are an investment. They require work. In this chapter, we discussed the following tools for maintaining healthy relationships:

- Managing expectations
- Reducing self-centeredness
- Emotional risk-taking
- Practicing forgiveness
- Adhering to a healthy use of boundaries
- Maintaining trust
- Showing appreciation

Our life is enriched by our relationships and we can be a blessing to others. Many times we are a blessing to others without even realizing it. Negotiating a balance between efforts put into maintaining your relationships while staying true to yourself will be ongoing, but totally worth the effort. Quality relationships are one of the keys to a happy, fulfilling life.

Your Turn:

In your interactions with others this week, spend time listening and focusing on someone. Ask follow-up questions to show interest.

Name of the person:
_____

What is your relationship to them:
_____

List a way you can follow through with showing this person that their interests are important to you:
_____

List the top three people in your life and their relationship to you. What is their love language?

#1. Name: _____

Relationship: _____

Love Language: _____

#2. Name: _____

Relationship: _____

Love Language: _____

#3. Name: _____

Relationship: _____

Love Language: _____

"Pray as though everything depends on God. Work as though everything depends on you."

- Saint Augustine

Chapter 11

Living in God's Will: Listening to the Lord

I hope you appreciate the life God has given you. When you awaken in the morning, thank Him for another day of existence, but don't stop there. Thank God for another day to spread His word and be a blessing to others. Knowing what actions to take in order to be a blessing to others may not always be clear, so we must ask Him to show us the way.

Self-Centered

Are you selfish? This may appear to be a harsh question, perhaps I should ask, instead, if you are self-centered. Self-centeredness is merely a polite way to say selfish. In writing a book about living your life to the fullest, I feel as though this is a selfish endeavor. In a way it is, because you are checking items off your bucket list and fulfilling your goals.

Hopefully, these are goals which you have prayed over and are pleasing to the Lord.

In scripture, we are told to take the focus off of ourselves and place it on others. "Don't be selfish; don't try to impress others. Be humble, thinking of others as better than yourselves. Don't look out only for your own interests, but take on interest in others, too." (Philippians 2:3-4 NLT) I like the way this tells us not to try to impress others. Your goals should be for the benefit of you and God, not so you can have bragging rights in the office or on social media.

In his book entitled *Don't Waste Your Life*, John Piper reports "We must make sacrificial life choices rooted in the assurance that magnifying Christ through generosity and mercy is more satisfying than selfishness". I find this quote to be quite profound, so I will break it down according to my interpretation. It starts by stating that making sacrifices is a choice we make. These sacrifices will be more satisfying to us than remaining selfish. Basically, when we help others, we end up helping ourselves. It talks about us needing to be generous and merciful to others. For some, generosity is a way of life while for others it is a conscious decision. In this effort to avoid being selfish, it does not mean you should not check things off your bucket list, or try to attain your goals. Quite the contrary. Some of these items on your list should be charitable. Yes, you may have possessions, high-end items if that is your desire. You must also be willing to give up your possessions. You must be willing to share. That beautiful designer purse should not be your idol. It's great to live out your dreams and to have nice things, but make sure your life does not revolve solely around you and your desires. If your goal is to have a nice home, I hope it is so you can open that home up to others.

The Prayer Reveal

When designing your goals, it should involve prayer. Ask God to reveal His will for your life. When going to God in prayer, be patient and listen for His response. It helps to write down what you hear. It may be difficult to distinguish, at the moment, whether it is God you are hearing. Reviewing these written notes during a time of reflection can bring clarity to your situation. When in doubt, ask yourself "Would this be pleasing to the Lord?" Really spend the time with God. It can become an easy habit to say a quick daily prayer without listening to what God may have to tell you.

Being raised Catholic and attending parochial school, it became drilled in me to say prayers and give thanks to God. We go to church services to hear the Word of God through Bible scripture and the message provided by our pastors. Do you take the time to pause after prayer and listen to what God is personally telling you? This is an area I myself am working on. Sometimes, I may have a moment of personal reflection that occurs during a Sunday sermon, then the service ends, and off I go to my busy life. Many times, I do not reflect upon the message again until maybe the following week when attending services. (I'm sure my pastor will not be thrilled by hearing this, but I'm being honest, to hold myself accountable.) Have that conversation with God and remember, conversations involve both talking and listening. In her book *How To Age Without Getting Old,* Joyce

Myer states, "When we learn to discern what God is giving us the grace to do and what we do not have His grace to do, we can save ourselves much difficulty". Pay attention to what God is revealing in your life.

How to be a Good Person

What does it mean to be a good person? When I think of a good person, I think of someone honest, ethical, kind, and giving in terms of both their time and resources. They are soft-spoken, slow to anger, and never involved in drama. This person always agrees to help, stays late, and of course, is a hospitable host. This person does the right thing and encourages others to do so as well. Donating to charities, and helping others out financially are also activities that come to mind. A good person spreads joy and provides hope and encouragement to others. Are you a good person? Sure, we would all love to be this good person, but it is not realistic. We are flesh and blood, mortal beings. When assessing whether you are a good person, does your response depend upon the feedback you receive from others, what you read in the Bible, or hear at church? On the other hand, is your assessment based on self-examination of your own soul? When you observe others, do you judge whether they are a good person? How do you make this determination? Certainly, you cannot afford to donate to every person who asks for help. Our resources of money and time are finite. We are not perfect so there will be times when we act out of the flesh. Only you will know what giving your best self looks like.

Having the Heart of a Servant

According to Matthew 20:28, Jesus states "...for even I, the Son of Man, came here not to be served but to serve others, and to give my life as a ransom for many." (NLT) Being of service to others, just as Christ did for us, is an honor. Do you have the heart of a servant? Having a servant's heart involves sacrifice. Sometimes these sacrifices will be intentional in order to help others, other times, these sacrifices will be thrust upon us. According to Joel Osteen in his book *Blessed in the Darkness*, "Sometimes God will inconvenience you in order to help somebody else. Instead of getting frustrated when our plans don't work out, we need to remember it's not all about us". A good reminder to keep us humble is to remember that it is not all about you. It means being loving and many times this loving behavior must be towards those who are acting unlovable. This kind of selfless behavior is pleasing to the Lord.

> A good reminder to keep us humble is to remember that it is not all about you.

Being a Christian includes doing things the Lord would approve of. The Bible tells us we cannot get to Heaven by good deeds alone. Therefore, being a good person and a Christian are not mutually exclusive. I have found there to be many good people in this world who, I was disappointed to discover, were not Christian. Such a waste. Just because these people were not Christian did not mean they were not good people. It hurts to think I will not be in Heaven with them. In my thoughts, although selfish, I compare it to working hard for the paycheck that is never received.

According to (Acts 20:24 NLT), "But my life is worth nothing to me unless I use it for finishing the work assigned me by the Lord Jesus—the work of telling others the Good News about the wonderful grace of God." Our lives really are not our own. God put us here to perform a task. For many of us, determining that task can be a hurdle in itself.

> Being a good person and a Christian are not mutually exclusive.

This book is about living your life to the fullest as a Christian. So, in my opinion, being a good person in the eyes of the Lord would mean bringing as many people to Christ as possible. Bringing people to Christ is not easy. The devil is on high alert in this area. He does not want conversions to Christianity. Bringing people to Christ can feel overwhelming. It involves sharing Scripture, inviting and bringing people to church, as well as discussing the Lord and our blessings whenever possible. It also involves living a life that is Christ-like. These days, more than ever, we are being watched. People observe how we react to life events. They can see if we have Christ in our hearts. Being a role model is one of the best ways we can display our Christianity. We can also take advantage of any opportunities to praise our Lord. Someone compliments us on our weight loss, and we can respond, "I owe it all to the Lord for helping me through those rough days". You get that raise and report "I prayed for this, and God delivered!" Give the Lord the praise He deserves. Use any excuse to give God the glory. Our purpose here on Earth is to glorify the Lord. Suppose you found the cure for cancer, would you keep it all to yourself or would you share it with the world?

Of course, you would share it so you could save lives. Sharing our belief in Christ is the same thing. Why would you want to keep such information to yourself? Think of how horrible it would be to make it to Heaven only to realize you could have brought others with you.

> **Think About It:**
> **Do you care what other people think about you?**

Fitting Into Society

Do you base your sense of self-worth on society? Social media has a strong hold over most of us. Do you find yourself needing validation from others? Does that ping of a text message make you feel important? When posting on social media do you go back to see how many likes or comments you receive? What if no one likes or comments? Do you delete it? If so, how long do you wait for people to respond? When leaving the house looking good, do you seek approval from others in the form of compliments? If you were not to receive compliments, would it change how you dress or style your hair? Think of the times when you heard someone say they made a quick trip to the store looking like a mess and then ran into everyone they knew. This is when I usually hear people say "I don't care what people think" referring to their sense of self-confidence. Wanting to be a unique individual is a sign of maturity, unless of course it is done to garnish attention. Do you care what others think of you? Would it bother you being called a "Jesus Freak" or a "Holy

Roller"? Do you listen to Christian music in the car with the windows rolled down? We shouldn't care if people call us a Jesus Freak. After all, if you're going to be a freak it might as well be a Jesus Freak! Never tone down your love of the Lord.

Self-Care and Helping Others

Being a good person is about where your focus is. Self-care is a buzzword used commonly today. It refers to taking care of yourself and was originally intended for caregivers: mothers taking care of small children, adults taking care of their elderly parents, you get the idea. It was aimed at selfless people who focused so much on the needs of others, their own needs took a backseat. I am sure you have heard the familiar scenario of being in a plane when there is a change in cabin pressure: the oxygen mask drops and you are instructed to put the mask on yourself first before helping others. Ironically, so many people need to be reminded that they cannot properly aid others if they do not help themselves first. We do not have to be feeling at our absolute best to be useful. Many people use the excuse that if they are not at their best, they are no good to others. Actually, it is when we are *not* at our best, that we *should* help others. Helping others can give us a sense of purpose, not to mention that warm, fuzzy feeling that comes from knowing you have made someone else's life a little better. For example, many people like to take church mission trips. Some people go to third-world countries and return posting pictures of themselves with little Haitian children. They get "oohs" and "aahs" from their online friends as well as comments praising them for their good deeds. They have helped people during their trip; however, I believe the ones receiving the greatest benefit were themselves. People return from mission trips changed for the better. I am not saying you should not go on a mission trip. As a matter of fact, it is on my own Christian bucket list. I am saying that if you do go, please do it for the right reasons.

Are you a self-sacrificing person or the self-centered type? If you are a self-sacrificing person, then you will need to make time for self-care. If, on the other hand, you are the self-centered type then make sure to check your motives. It is human nature to focus on yourself first. It simply means you will need to consciously focus on ways to assist others. Ask yourself who your focus is on: Is it solely on yourself? Is it on another person? Is any of that focus on the Lord? Those of you who tend to be self-centered may shift from total focus on self to focus on self and your inner circle. Those of you who tend to be natural caregivers may want to reach out further by focusing on serving in the community and being globally conscious.

I'm a Good Person...

Most people will report being a good person. Usually, this statement is accompanied by a list of justifications such as being a courteous driver, purchasing fundraising items sold by children, contributing to church bake sales, etc. If this is you, that's wonderful, but please don't stop there. Being a good person is like being at your ideal weight. It is not something you can say you have attained and then not monitor it. Life is constantly changing and can throw us for a loop. The enemy will make sure to put obstacles in our path. Challenge yourself. If this year you contributed to the church bake sale, then how about next year offering to work it or better yet, be in charge of it! If you realize you fall short of being a good person, no need to fret, just work on it. Do some deep soul-searching to determine the reasoning behind your thoughts. Being a good person is not always about donating money. After all, we only have so much money we can donate. If we give too much away, we may default on our own financial obligations. This is truly about giving of ourselves with a kind, open heart.

The Good Person Bucket List

As you may have already noticed, I enjoy creating lists. Here are some of my ideas as to what a good person's bucket list looks like. Keep in mind these are general ideas. Your life situation is unique, so your activities will look different. Hopefully, you will be inspired to create your own list of meaningful activities.

1. Adopt a shelter dog
2. Become a foster parent
3. Donate blood and/or plasma
4. Visit with the elderly
5. Help an elderly neighbor with home repairs
6. Become an organ donor
7. Volunteer consistently, for at least 6 months
8. Share your lunch with someone

9. Invite and take someone to church with you
10. Give a personalized Bible as a gift
11. Give a cross necklace as a gift
12. Serve at church
13. Go on a mission trip
14. Anonymously help a co-worker
15. Carry jumper cables to help motorists
16. Learn CPR
17. Shop local to support small business owners
18. Post a positive review of a business
19. Tell someone how much you appreciate them
20. Always say please and thank you

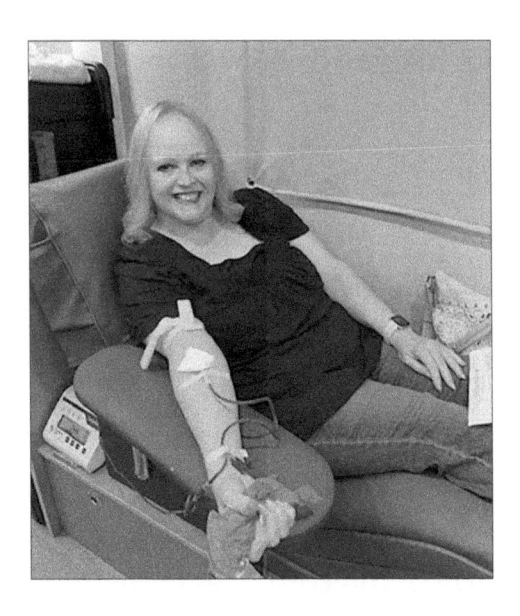

Your Mission

In his famous book, *A Purpose Driven Life*, Rick Warren discussed having both a mission and a ministry. He distinguished between the two by reporting "Your ministry is your service to believers, and your mission is your service to unbelievers". I never really thought of it in this manner. We can serve at our church, and we should, but we are "singing to the choir" when we do this. These are people who are already saved. We also need to go out in the world and find lost souls. Reverend Warren continues to state, "Your mission is a continuation of Jesus' mission on earth. As his followers, we are to continue what Jesus started". I think this is a beautiful way to frame our works of service. Serving at our home church is vital. It provides a sense of community. We need to uplift and encourage our church family. If you are just starting out in your Christian journey, this is the perfect place to begin. Through your ministry, you will learn how to best reach out to nonbelievers. Say a prayer for your mission to be revealed to you.

Mission–serving unbelievers	Ministry–serving the church (believers)
Grace–that which is given which you do not deserve	Mercy–forgiveness given which you do not deserve

"And we know that in all things God works for the good of those who love him, who have been called according to his purpose." (Romans 8:28 NIV) Do not wait for opportunities to share your love of the Lord, create them! Show your love for the Lord. He has a purpose for each one of us.

Living in God's Will: Listening to the Lord

Your Turn:

Spend 30 minutes with God. Set a timer. Be intentional with this prayer time. Praise the Lord and give Him thanks for all the blessings He has bestowed upon you. Make your requests known to Him and then listen for His voice. Write down His response.

What did you give the Lord praise and thanks for?
_____
_____

What did you request of Him?
_____
_____

Who did you pray for?
_____
_____

What did He reveal to you?
_____
_____

> *"A bad attitude is like a flat tire.*
> *You won't get anywhere until you change it."*
>
> -Unknown

Chapter 12

Are We There Yet?: Enjoying the Journey

It is the phrase every parent has heard from the backseat of the car "Are we there yet?" Most of the time, along our journey, we continue to ask if we are near our destination. Often it seems as if we will just never make it there, especially if we have never been there before. We have inquiries, such as once we arrive, will it have been worth all the effort? Then, of course, "I'm here, now what do I do?" Having questions and apprehension toward the future shows that you are trying to plan ahead by anticipating the consequences of your actions. We often feel that once we reach our goals, we will be happy. Happiness is a constant journey and obtaining it is totally up to you.

What Is Success?

Sometimes we get so busy with our daily tasks, we don't realize how truly well we are doing. We don't always enjoy, or appreciate, the process of growth. I cannot emphasize enough the importance of self-reflection in our lives. Take a minute to stop and reflect upon your current journey. Make self-reflection a daily practice for yourself. Too many people wait for others to thrust this reflection upon them. The Thanksgiving table has caused many a single person to reevaluate their dating strategy. Don't let Aunt Ida be the reason you decided to start a family. Take responsibility for your own journey.

Most people want to be considered a success but who defines success? Some people try to earn the respect of a particular person such as a parent or supervisor. This can be detrimental to one's self-esteem. There are just some people out there who cannot be pleased. If we wait on the approval of others, then we are giving our power away to them. It feels great when we receive accolades from that hard-to-please person, but please don't fall into that trap. If you want to meet up to high expectations, let it be your own high expectations. Do not depend on others to raise your self-esteem. It is your job to feel good about yourself. It is a matter of self-respect. Success looks different at the various stages of our lives. Your definition of success may be different from your family members' definition. It is not possible to escape yourself, so make sure you are being true to yourself. What does being true to yourself look like? It means setting and adhering to boundaries so you feel good about yourself.

Goal Attainment and Beyond

What happens when you attain a goal? Do you have a sense of accomplishment? Happiness? Contentment? Perhaps relief? Maybe you have the feeling that anything is possible. You should feel proud of yourself. You stretched yourself and worked hard and it paid off. Perhaps, you don't have that great feeling. After all the planning, hard work, and waiting, you are left feeling as if "It's about time already". It can feel anticlimactic to reach a goal. You may even feel a little depressed. It is not uncommon for performers to feel deflated the morning after a big show. After months of rehearsals and practice the "big day" is now over. No more hanging out with friends during rehearsals or feelings of anticipation. It is enjoyable to have something to look forward to. Having reached your goal, you may be asking "Now what?"

Once you reach a goal it is time to set your next goal. This goal may be an extension of your first goal by taking things a step further. For example, if graduating college was the initial goal then obtaining employment or becoming certified/licensed in your field could be the extension goal. Maybe you feel good about some physical goals you have just achieved and your next goal is to help others attain similar results. Maybe you decide you now want to focus on financial goals. We should always have something we are striving toward. We need a reason to wake up in the morning. Sometimes it can be frustrating when we attain a goal, we were excited about and then find it difficult to set equally exciting follow-up goals. Be intentional about setting these follow-up goals. It is important to have goals you are invested in.

When reaching a goal, there may be trial and error in terms of creating our next goal. This is fine as long as you continue with self-reflection. You may start on a goal and realize you really don't care about it as much as you initially thought you would. For example, you may be planning a trip to France and decide the goal of learning to speak French seems worthwhile. After a few weeks of French lessons, you may decide it is boring and not worth all that effort for a ten-day vacation. That's okay. Not every goal will be attained. The process of starting work on your goal and the realization that it is not for you are learning experiences within themselves. You do, however, want to make certain you are not merely rationalizing yourself out of the hard work required to meet a goal. A common example of this is dieting. People often rationalize themselves out of dietary restrictions with such statements as "Well, people need to accept me for who I am" and "An extra few pounds is not going to make a difference".

When you set a goal ask yourself why you are setting this goal. "Why do I want to lose weight?" "Why do I want to coach the little league baseball team?" The more specific the answer to the "Why" question, the more dedication you will have toward achieving it. An answer such as "It would be cool" is not one that tells me there will be a lot of commitment behind it. Take time to develop your next goal and enjoy the process of working through it!

> **Think About It:**
> **Does thinking about your goal make you smile?**

Attitude

Attitude, isn't this just a bunch of fluff? We are frequently told we need to have a positive attitude. I never hear people say a bad attitude is the way to go. An attitude is your response to life events. You are given a new task at work. Is your attitude that of resistance or do you embrace the opportunity for a challenge? When going out socially, are you difficult to please or easygoing? Attitude is a way of thinking often reflected through one's behavior and mannerisms. When faced with a challenge, you may whine, complain, and resist dealing with the work involved, yet with the same dilemma, a peer may respond in an excited manner, viewing the challenge as a way to compete with one's self. Same challenge, different attitude. Either way, the challenge must be dealt with. Which person would you rather be?

Our attitude can easily be influenced by our emotions. Sometimes, however, our attitude is determined by our physical condition as well. Have you ever responded abruptly to someone because you were hungry? Made hurtful comments when you were angered? Expressed feelings of defeat out of loneliness? Or showed a lack of enthusiasm because you were tired? There is an acronym frequently used as a self-coaching tool in the social work field regarding how we are influenced in both our decision-making process as well as our attitude, it is HALT (Hungry, Angry, Lonely, Tired). These are the situations in which we can find ourselves vulnerable in terms of making choices, including our attitude, due to physical and/or emotional occurrences. When we are aware of these stressors, we can actively make positive choices, such as the attitude we display, rather than by default due to physical and/or emotional issues. I recommend using HALT as a tool to take the time to identify triggers to your attitude choices.

It is important to keep our attitude positive because negative attitudes can keep us from receiving blessings. Joyce Meyer in her book, *The Power of Thank You*, reminds us that "Complaining prevented many Israelites from entering the Promised Land. Perhaps we should think about this a little more deeply and consider whether our complaining is keeping us from some of the blessings God wants to give us". Think about your children. When they whine and complain, do you really want to reward them for this behavior? Of course not! When people are appreciative of us, however, we want to bless them. When we think of what would be pleasing to the Lord, we should think of praise, worship, and gratitude. Complaining and lamenting over our circumstances will not help us to feel better.

We start new endeavors full of excitement, hope, and anticipation. We plan on doing our best. This enthusiasm, however, will eventually wane. As we get into the work involved, challenges happen, tasks take longer than anticipated, and slowly discouragement creeps in. As we get discouraged, our attitude begins to decline. We may not even realize this is happening. To accomplish goals, we often must engage in monotonous tasks. Oftentimes, these tasks can leave us with a mundane attitude. If we continue with our self-reflection exercises, we should be able to catch ourselves from falling into this downward spiral.

Our Inner Dialogue

We have thoughts constantly going through our minds. Do you ever think about what you are thinking about? The term metacognition means the "awareness and understanding of one's own thought processes". Even when we are sitting silently in a lecture, at a church sermon, or watching television, as focused as you may think you are, your mind is reacting and interpreting. We make predictions in our minds as to where the preacher is leading us. Comments we hear spark ideas within us. We have an inner dialogue that directs our outward actions. It can be difficult to turn off these thoughts. This inner dialogue can build us up or tear us down. Meditation and yoga can be used to slow down racing thoughts in order to become focused on one issue at a time.

> Inner dialogue can build us up or tear us down.

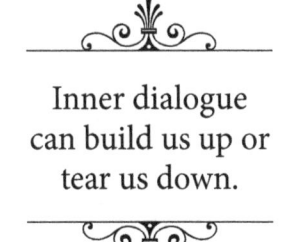

In the 1930s, a French entomologist by the name of August Magnan reported it was "aerodynamically impossible" for the bee to fly due to its heavy body and light wings. Despite this assertion, we all know the bee does, in fact, fly. How? Why? This reminds me of a motivational lecture I attended many years ago, where I heard a story about the bumblebee. According to the story, no one told the bumblebee it was physically impossible for him to fly. He was unaware of these limitations, so he flew anyway. This story was used as an analogy to remind us that negative thoughts limit us therefore, we need to open our minds to all possibilities. How far would you push yourself if you felt you could do anything? Since hearing this story, as I stated many years ago, more research has been conducted on the bee and I am sure evidence will be found to support the reasoning for Mr. Bumblebee's flight. For me, I prefer the analogy. I prefer to think about ways to stop my negative thoughts. I don't know about you, but I certainly don't want to limit myself.

In his book, *Winning the War in Your Mind*, Craig Groeschel reports "Whether it's self-doubts or worrying or responding poorly to a bad day or a tough season in life, we all wrestle with negative thoughts that try to hijack our emotions and decisions". He suggests conducting a "thought audit" in order to give yourself an idea of what your thought life is actually like. I love this idea. Much like going to the doctor for a physical where you get weighed and have blood work completed to determine your physical health, in conducting your thought audit, you are becoming aware of the type of thoughts that are popping into your mind to determine your emotional health.

What kind of thoughts are going through your mind? Take an inventory of these thoughts. I know there are too many to document all of them. Record them in general terms. For instance, on Sunday when you were in church, what was going on in your mind? While driving to work today, what were you thinking about? We often get a glimpse into our friends' thought lives when we get together through the topics of conversation being discussed. Maybe when you are with friends, you don't discuss what is on your mind because you don't want to worry them or you prefer to keep it positive so as to uplift them, thus embracing the "Fake it till you make it" mentality. Try for three days to write down what you are thinking about during various times of the day. Look at that list and decide whether those thoughts are uplifting or negative. The enemy will often try to give us doubts, worries, and self-deprecating thoughts. Ask yourself if these thoughts are from God or the enemy. God will provide you with thoughts of encouragement for your self-improvement. Think of your response to your thoughts. Are these thoughts bringing you closer to or further away from the Lord?

Positive Affirmations

Affirmations are reminders to yourself, from yourself, stating that you are a capable individual. Using affirmations can help to reduce anxiety and provide encouragement. One of my favorites is "I can do hard things!" It helps me push forward and I use this affirmation especially when I am doing activities out of my comfort zone. Using positive affirmations can help provide a feeling of independence. This is important because we should not rely on other people to influence our attitude. When we have a good attitude, it helps us to move forward quickly and use less energy because we are not fighting the process. When we have a positive outlook, it can help us to finish unpleasant, although necessary, tasks.

Here are some examples of positive affirmations you can use to pump up your attitude and keep you headed in the direction of your goals. You can practice these, but I suggest their use as a springboard for creating your own personalized affirmations.

1. I can do hard things.
2. I am getting better every day.
3. I am good at setting and maintaining boundaries.
4. I can choose to be happy today.
5. I am unique. I do not need to compete with anyone.
6. I am a good problem solver.
7. I appreciate and respect my body.
8. I can control my reaction to outside situations.
9. I trust in God's timing.
10. I do not have to be perfect to be a blessing to others.

You Are a Mirror

Attitudes are contagious. A few minutes with a negative Nancy and the next thing you know, your motivation has dwindled. Then there's those smiling, peppy people who seem to make everything seem exciting. Who would you rather be around? Sure, there are times when misery loves company and everyone needs some time to vent, but for the most part, we want to be around encouraging people. I'm not talking about the phony "let's do this" type of people, who are pretending to be encouraging, I'm referring to genuinely positive individuals. What type of person are you? Do you encourage others? It's not enough to just be positive about meeting our own goals, we should be encouraging to others. Think about the people in your life. Who are the individuals providing you with encouragement, either on purpose or indirectly? You should be cheerleading for them as well. Can you remember the last time you encouraged someone?

Your attitude is a mirror to the world. As a Christian, we are being looked at in both our actions and attitudes. This can be an uncomfortable position to be in because we are human and will, therefore, not be perfect, yet we must be role models for others. There will be times when we are discouraged or feel negative, but we cannot always give into it. We must acknowledge these feelings for our own mental health, but we cannot linger in such negativity. Brainstorming solutions to a problem can be productive, however, ruminating on problems can become a negative habit. We need to remain emotionally healthy by focusing on positive and productive thoughts.

Gratitude

According to Lesowitz and Sammons in their book *Living Life As A Thank You*, "Gratitude makes us healthier." This is no surprise. They continue on to state that "Experts now tell us that giving thanks makes us happier and more resilient, and it strengthens our relationships and reduces our stress". How often do you think about your answered prayers? When concentrating on goal attainment it is easy to focus on what we do not have—yet. It is easy to think about that trip you cannot afford or an opportunity that did not come your way.

A Sunday in church or a television story concentrating on the disadvantaged is sure to bring some humility to the soul. There will always be people who are doing better than us and there will always be people who are worse off. To be successful in attaining our goals, it is important to surround oneself with positive role models, individuals who are at the level of success you are striving towards. In doing this, however, it leaves us in a position of always wanting more and thus compromising our ability to be appreciative, *if* we are not careful. Show gratitude that you have these role models in your life. Thank God for leading you in the direction of your goals. Prioritize your thoughts of gratitude.

Are you a grateful person? According to Robert Emmons, in his book *Thanks!*, "Research has shown that grateful people experience higher levels of positive emotions such as joy, enthusiasm, love, happiness, and optimism and that the practice of gratitude as a discipline protects a person from the destructive impulses of envy, resentment, greed, and bitterness". I like the fact that gratitude is being thought of as a discipline. It is not something that may come naturally. With practice, however, we can learn to think in terms of gratitude. It is difficult to be bitter when we are counting our blessings. Are you appreciative of what you have? It is so easy to focus on what we are missing. Sometimes we forget to be grateful for what we do have. When we view gratitude as a protective factor, we can learn to incorporate it into our lifestyle just as if it were prayer or brushing our teeth or eating our veggies. When you pray and spend time with the Lord, do you thank him for those answered prayers?

Do you tithe? Tithing is giving God the first ten percent of your income. He is the one who gives you the ability to earn that income and is only asking for the first ten percent of it. In my opinion, tithing is a form of gratitude. "Remember this: Whoever sows sparingly will also reap sparingly, and whoever sows generously will also reap generously. Each of you should give what you have decided in your heart to give, not reluctantly or under compulsion, for God loves a cheerful giver." (2 Corinthians 9:6-7 NIV) In giving, of course, we usually think in terms of finances, such as tithing and then giving to charity. We can also think in terms of service. Being generous to others with our time can also be seen as gratitude. If we are going to give, we may as well do so cheerfully rather than grudgingly. Either way, you will be giving so why not do so with a kind heart? We are all limited in our resources, be it time or money, therefore, we need to do so with intentionality. When you give your time to others, make it quality time. Regardless of what you give, give it your all, don't be stingy with your gifts! No one likes the ungrateful, especially our Heavenly Father. He wants us to appreciate what He has given us.

"I am not saying this because I am in need, for I have learned to be content whatever the circumstances. I know what it is to be in need, and I know what it is to have plenty. I have learned the secret of being content in any and every situation, whether well fed or hungry, whether living in plenty or in want." (Philippians 4:11-12 NIV) There will always be a part of you striving for more. That little bit extra. You may want a more pleasing house, career, family relationship, or physique. It reminds me of that children's book *If You Give A*

Mouse A Cookie. In case you are not familiar, this book basically shows us that regardless of how generous someone may be to us, we will always crave more. Acknowledge your desires for "more" while being appreciative. Give God thanks and praise for what you do have. "Always giving thanks to God the Father for everything, in the name of our Lord Jesus Christ." (Ephesians 5:20 NIV)

A Prayer Journal

Do you journal? Some people find that expressing their emotions in written form helps them to cope with their emotions and stress. Writing out their thoughts and feelings, as well as situations they are encountering, can be cathartic. Some people will find they need to journal daily. Others may only need to do so on a weekly basis. It all depends on what you are going through in your life. Regardless of whether or not you express your thoughts and feelings, be sure to record your prayers to God. You may even wish to have a separate book for your prayers. Date these prayers and requests to God. Leave room to the side of your prayers so you can go back later and make notes. Review this prayer book from time to time. It is interesting to see how God responds to our requests. When you notice an answered prayer, use that space to document it. It is a special feeling to see your prayers being answered. We have become such an immediate gratification society, that when we do not see instant responses, we think nothing is happening. I find it amazing how God is always working in the background for us. He is lining things up for us that we cannot visualize in the moment and then, in His own timing, He grants our requests. Sometimes when our prayers are answered, they do not look the way we envisioned them. Do not try to force your will. Pray that God's will be done. God's will for us is so much better than anything we can imagine. This is another reason documenting in our prayer journals is so important. I hope you will give this a try. This is not a quick fix; it will take time to see how your prayers and God's responses evolve. You will not be disappointed.

> God's will for us is so much better than anything we can imagine.

As we end the last chapter of this book, I want you to reflect on the positive factors in your life. We cannot change our past and we are not promised tomorrow. Think about what you are grateful for today and say a prayer of praise to God for what he has given you. Share with others how God has blessed your life. Living your best life is living a life of gratitude. To be truly happy entails being appreciative of God's blessings. So go out there and crush those goals, tackle that bucket list, and make a difference in the lives of others. Live your best life while embracing your Christianity!

Your Turn:

Thinking about the past week, list five things you are grateful for.

1._____

2._____

3._____

4._____

5._____

List three people you are grateful to have in your life.

1._____

2._____

3._____

NOTES

Chapter 1

Mcleod, Saul. "Maslow's Hierarchy of Needs." Simply Psychology. Last modified July 26, 2023. https://www.simplypsychology.org/maslow.html.

Menendez, Alicia. *The Likeability Trap: How to Break Free and Succeed as You Are*, 150 New York, NY: HarperCollins, 2019.

"A Quote by Michael Jordan." Goodreads | Meet Your Next Favorite Book. Accessed June 21, 2024. https://www.goodreads.com/quotes/38639-some-people-want-it-to-happen-some-wish-it-would.

Rev. Roberts, John W. "Far From Home?" Speech, Grace Presbyterian Church Sunday Sermon, Corpus Christi, TX, January 14, 2024.

"Watch Dick Clark's New Year's Rockin' Eve with Ryan Seacrest TV Show—ABC.com." ABC. Accessed July 26, 2024. https://abc.com/show/91f771e2-8def-4aac-8aad-473575b2f5dc.

Chapter 2

Erikson, Erik H., and Joan M. Erikson. *The Life Cycle Completed (Extended Version)*, 114. New York: W. W. Norton & Company, 1998.

JulianBlogs. ""Comparison Is The Thief of Joy"." Medium. Last modified December 1, 2023. https://medium.com/self-reflection-philosophy/comparison-is-the-thief-of-joy-168fe60a15f0.

"A Quote by Roy T. Bennett." Goodreads | Meet Your Next Favorite Book. Accessed June 21, 2024. https://www.goodreads.com/quotes/7735958-if-you-don-t-know-who-you-truly-are-you-ll-never.

Chapter 3

"A Quote by Albert Einstein." Goodreads | Meet Your Next Favorite Book. Accessed July 4, 2024. https://www.goodreads.com/quotes/29213-life-is-like-riding-a-bicycle-to-keep-your-balance.

"A Quote from The Light in the Heart." Goodreads | Meet Your Next Favorite Book. Accessed July 29, 2024. https://www.goodreads.com/quotes/7987120-the-past-is-a-place-of-reference-not-a-place.

Chapter 4

"Attention Required!" Attention Required! | Cloudflare. Accessed July 4, 2024. https://www.peacecorps.gov/about-the-agency/.

Campbell, Courtney. "Which State Really Has the World's Largest Ball of Twine?" Wide Open Country. Last modified September 26, 2020. https://www.wideopencountry.com/biggest-ball-of-twine/.

Christ Church Shrewsbury – Episcopal – Shrewsbury, NJ – Founded 1702. Accessed July 29, 2024. https://christchurchshrewsbury.org/wp-content/uploads/2017/07/8-August-ML-article-for-Web-Site.pdf.

Lieu, A. "George H.W. Bush loved to skydive, took last Jump for 90th birthday." Fox News. Last modified December 1, 2018. https://www.foxnews.com/us/george-h-w-bush-loved-to-skydive-took-last-one-for-90th-birthday.

"Our mission." Make-A-Wish America. n.d. https://wish.org/mission.

The Bucket List. Directed by R Reiner. 2007. Warner Brothers, Movie.

Rev. John W. Roberts. *Caught Red Handed: Little Moments When God Showed Up Big*. Independently published, 2022.

Running of the Bulls 2025 | Pamplona Bull Run 2025. Last modified January 14, 2020. https://www.runningofthebulls.com/.

"S4.E21: A List Before Dying." Yes Dear. Directed by J Meyer. Columbia Broadcasting System, May 3, 2004.

"Vending machine – Ms. Pearl: The giant squirrel statue in Texas." Ms. Pearl: The Giant Squirrel Statue in Texas. n.d. https://berdollsquirrel.com/vending-machine/.

Venegas, Mauricio. "World's Largest Fork in Springfield is the Site of a Million Selfies." Columbia Missourian. Last modified June 13, 2019. https://www.columbiamissourian.com/special_section/tourism/southwest_missouri/worlds-largest-fork-in-springfield-is-the-site-of-a-million-selfies/article_fbf45648-65d9-11e9-a564-c7c948351e54.html.

Chapter 5

Duperrin, Bertrand. "We Always Overestimate the Change That Will Occur in the Next Two Years…." Bertrand Duperrin's Notepad. Last modified October 16, 2018. https://www.duperrin.com/english/2018/11/08/we-always-overestimate-the-change-that-will-occur-in-the-next-two-years/.

Foy, Terri S. *Dream It–Pin It–Live It: Make Vision Boards Work for You,* 45. Austin, Texas: The Fedd Agency, Inc, 2015.

"Frequency Illusion." Psychology Today. Accessed July 25, 2024. https://www.psychologytoday.com/us/basics/frequency-illusion.

Green, Crystal. *Visual Prayer: How to Create a Spiritual Vision Board, 2nd ed*. Houston, Texas: The Dream Life Foundation, 2016.

Quotespedia.org. "Die with Memories, Not Dreams. – Anonymous – Quotespedia.org." Quotespedia.org. Last modified April 9, 2020. https://www.quotespedia.org/authors/a/anonymous/die-with-memories-not-dreams-anonymous/#google_vignette.

Straw, Eli. *"Fear of Success & 3 Steps to Overcome It." Success Starts Within*. Last modified April 9, 2024. https://www.successstartswithin.com/sports-psychology-articles/fear-of-success-in-sports/fear-of-success/.

Chapter 6

Delonix, Kindal. "Www.quantumbooks.com." Www.quantumbooks.com. Last modified July 24, 2018. https://www.quantumbooks.com/home-and-family/personal-development/the-harvard-mba-study-on-goal-setting/.

Haughey, Duncan. "A Brief History of SMART Goals." Project Smart. Last modified December 13, 2014.

https://www.projectsmart.co.uk/smart-goals/brief-history-of-smart-goals.php#google_vignette.

Justice. "Create a Life You Don't Need a Vacation From: Quote (meaning) – Success Is Money." Success Is Money. Last modified December 12, 2020. https://successismoney.com/create-a-life-you-dont-need-a-vacation-from/.

Mcleod, Saul. "Maslow's Hierarchy of Needs." Simply Psychology. Last modified July 26, 2023. https://www.simplypsychology.org/maslow.html.

"S25.E5: Week 4." Dancing with the Stars. Burbank, CA: ABC Studios, August 27, 1997.

Tracy, Brian. *Goals!: How to Get Everything You Want — Faster Than You Ever Thought Possible, 2nd ed*, 33. Oakland, CA: Berrett-Koehler Publishers, 2010.

"Watch Hoarders Full Episodes, Video & More." A&E. Last modified January 15, 1970. https://www.aetv.com/shows/hoarders.

Chapter 7

"Betty White–Age, Health & Family." Biography. Last modified December 31, 2021. https://www.biography.com/actors/betty-white.

NOTES

Jakes, T. D. *Destiny: Step into Your Purpose*, 119. New York, NY: FaithWords, 2015.

"A Quote by Charles Buxton." Goodreads | Meet Your Next Favorite Book. Accessed June 23, 2024. https://www.goodreads.com/quotes/26920-you-will-never-find-time-for-anything-if-you-want.

Tracy, Brian. *Eat That Frog!: 21 Great Ways to Stop Procrastinating and Get More Done in Less Time*, 2nd ed., 33. San Francisco, CA: Berrett-Koehler Publishers, Inc., 2007.

"A Valuable Lesson For A Happier Life." YouTube. Last modified May 4, 2016. https://youtu.be/SqGRnlXplx0?si=x-PXBlAA5k0zrCf5.

Chapter 8

Clear, James. *Atomic Habits: An Easy & Proven Way to Build Good Habits & Break Bad Ones*, 46. London: Penguin Random House, LLC, 2018.

Guy-Evans, Olivia. "Pareto Principle (The 80-20 Rule): Examples & More." Simply Psychology. Last modified September 21, 2023. https://www.simplypsychology.org/pareto-principle.html.

Hitch. Directed by Andy Tennant. 2005. Seattle, WA: IMDbPro, 2005. Film.

Hyatt, Michael, and Daniel Harkavy. *Living Forward: A Proven Plan to Stop Drifting and Get the Life You Want*. Grand Rapids, Michigan: Baker Books, 2016.

Maxwell, John C. *Intentional Living: Choosing a Life That Matters*, 246. New York, NY: Center Street, 2015.

"Richie Norton Quotes (Author of The Power of Starting Something Stupid)." Goodreads | Meet Your Next Favorite Book. Accessed June 25, 2024. https://www.goodreads.com/author/quotes/5821896.Richie_Norton.

Witkiewitz, Katie, Corey R. Roos, Dana D. Colgan, and Sarah Bowen. *Mindfulness*, 1. Moston, MA: Hoegrefe Publishing Corporation, 2017.

Chapter 9

Cannon, Walter B. *Body Changes In Pain, Hunger, Fear And Rage: An Account Of Recent Researches Into The Functions Of Emotional Excitement*. New York, NY: D. Appleton and Co., 1915.

Creel, Bee. "Tempted To Skip Savasana? 10 Top Yoga Teachers Explain Why It's The Most Important Pose." Awaken. Last modified February 2, 2019. https://awaken.com/2019/02/tempted-to-skip-savasana-10-top-yoga-teachers-explain-why-its-the-most-important-pose/.

NOTES

Ellis, Albert. *Rational Emotive Behavior Therapy: It Works for Me—it Can Work for You*. Amherst, NY: Prometheus Books, 2004.

"Introvert Vs. Extrovert Personality: What's The Difference?" Simply Psychology. Last modified October 10, 2023. https://www.simplypsychology.org/introvert-extrovert.html.

McCain, John, and Mark Salter. *Why Courage Matters: The Way to a Braver Life*. New York, NY: Random House, Inc, 2004.

Meyer, Joyce. *Do It Afraid: Embracing Courage in the Face of Fear*, 8. New York, NY: FaithWords, 2020.

"A Quote by Napoleon Hill." Goodreads | Meet Your Next Favorite Book. Accessed June 28, 2024. https://www.goodreads.com/quotes/307339-do-not-wait-the-time-will-never-be-just-right.

"S4.E2: The One with the Cat." Friends. Burbank, CA: IMDb, October 2, 1997.

Storr, Anthony. *The Essential Jung*, 140-143. New York, NY: MJF Books, 1983.

Chapter 10

Chapman, Gary D. *The 5 Love Languages/Things I Wish I'd Known Before We Got Married*. Chicago, Illinois: Northfield Publishing, 2010.

Clinton, Hillary. "It Takes A Village." Speech, DNC Address, Chicago, Illinois, August 27, 1996.

"A Quote by Julia Roberts." Goodreads | Meet Your Next Favorite Book. Accessed June 25, 2024. https://www.goodreads.com/quotes/5937-you-know-it-s-love-when-all-you-want-is-that.

Chapter 11

Osteen, Joel. *Blessed in the Darkness: How All Things Are Working for Your Good*, 106. New York, NY: FaithWords, 2017.

Piper, John. *Don't Waste Your Life*, 107. Wheaton, Illinois: Crossway Bibles, 2003.

"A Quote by Augustine of Hippo." Goodreads | Meet Your Next Favorite Book. Accessed June 23, 2024. https://www.goodreads.com/quotes/377812-pray-as-though-every-thing-depends-on-god-and-work-as.

Warren, Rick. *The Purpose-driven Life: What on Earth Am I Here For?*, 355. Grand Rapids, Michigan: Zondervan, 2002.

Chapter 12

"A Bad Attitude Is Like A Flat Tire Quote?" Wheels Adviser. Last modified March 13, 2023. https://wheelsadviser.com/a-bad-attitude-is-like-a-flat-tire-quote/.

"Deciphering the Mystery of Bee Flight." Phys.org–News and Articles on Science and Technology. Last modified November 30, 2005. https://phys.org/news/2005-11-deciphering-mystery-bee-flight.html#google_vignette.

Emmons, Robert A. *Thanks!: How the New Science of Gratitude Can Make You Happier*, 11. Boston, MA: Houghton Mifflin Harcourt, 2007.

Groeschel, Craig. *Winning the War in Your Mind: Change Your Thinking, Change Your Life*, 21. Grand Rapids, Michigan: Zondervan, 2021.

Lesowitz, Nina, and Mary B. Sammons. *Living Life as a Thank You: The Transformative Power of Daily Gratitude*, xxiii. San Francisco, CA: Cleis Press Inc, 2009.

Meyer, Joyce. *The Power of Thank You: Discover the Joy of Gratitude*, 111. Murray, Kentucky: Faithwords, 2022.

Numeroff, Laura J. *If You Give a Mouse a Cookie*. New York, NY: HarperCollins, 1985.

About the Author

Sherry Koppal-Gilmore was born and raised in Maryland and found her way to South Texas to follow her dreams. As a licensed social worker and certified teacher, she always valued living life to the fullest. Sherry lives in Corpus Christi, Texas where she attends Grace Presbyterian Church, and uses her American Sign Language skills to broaden her student's horizons. In her free time, she enjoys traveling, Middle Eastern dancing, attending baseball games, and the occasional tug-of-war with her dog Bindi. For more information about Sherry, go to www.sherrykoppal-gilmore.com.